The
Science
of
Happiness

10 Principles for
Manifesting Your
Divine Nature

▼

RYUHO OKAWA

Destiny Books
Rochester, Vermont • Toronto, Canada

Destiny Books
One Park Street
Rochester, Vermont 05767
www.DestinyBooks.com

Destiny Books is a division of Inner Traditions International

The Science of Happiness is a compilation of *Kofuku-no-Genri* (The Principles of Happiness), *Satori-no-Genri* (The Principles of Enlightenment), and *Utopia-no-Genri* (The Principles of Utopia) originally published in 1990 in Japanese by IRH Press Co., Ltd, 1-6-7 Togoshi, Shinagawa-ku, Tokyo, 142-0041, Japan

Library of Congress Cataloging-in-Publication Data
Okawa, Ryuho, 1956–
  The science of happiness : 10 principles for manifesting your divine nature / Ryuho Okawa.
    p. cm.
  Includes translations from Japanese.
  Includes bibliographical references and index.
  ISBN 978-1-59477-320-4 (pbk.)
  1. Happiness—Religious aspects. 2. Kofuku no Kagaku (Organization)—Spiritual life. I. Okawa, Ryuho, 1956– Kofuku no genri. English. II. Okawa, Ryuho, 1956– Satori no genri. English. III. Okawa, Ryuho, 1956– Yutopia no genri. English. IV. Title.
  BP605.K55O334 2009
  299'.93—dc22
                                                                          2009018115

Printed and bound in the United States by Lake Book Manufacturing

10 9 8 7 6 5 4 3 2

Text design and layout by Priscilla Baker
This book was typeset in Garamond Premier Pro with Avant Garde used as a display typeface

Contents

◀ PART ONE ▶
The Dawn of the New Era

◀ PART TWO ▶
True Awakening

◀ PART THREE ▶
The Creation of an Ideal World

Introducing the Science of Happiness

Master Ryuho Okawa is a spiritual leader and contemporary vision-ary, well known for his wisdom, compassion, and commitment to edu-cating people to think and act in a spiritual way. In the tradition of Shakyamuni Buddha, Jesus, Confucius, and Moses, he teaches the prin-ciples that will bring people true happiness and open the path to a new and better age.

In March 1981, Ryuho Okawa was pursuing a career in business when he began to receive revelations from heavenly spirits who had been outstanding Buddhist monks in their previous lives.* He continued his studies and, after graduating with a law degree from the University of Tokyo that spring, was hired by a Japanese trading company. In 1982, he was transferred to the company's headquarters in New York, where he continued to receive revelations from high spirits. When Okawa returned to Japan, his spiritual communications expanded to include messages from Socrates, Isaac Newton, Abraham Lincoln, Florence Nightingale, Thomas Edison, Mahatma Gandhi, Helen Keller, and Pablo Picasso. Although still working for the trading company, he continued to

---

*March 23, 1981, is the day when he attained the great enlightenment and clearly realized the existence of spirits and the spirit world. That is the day he became "Master." For more information on his experience, please see chapter 1 of *Love, Nurture, and Forgive*.

gather knowledge about the spirit world and explore the eternal truths of life and the physical world. In August 1985, after four years of exploration, Master Ryuho Okawa began to publish books presenting the spiritual messages he had been receiving.

In July 1986, Master Okawa finally renounced his business career, and three months later he founded Happy Science (*Kofuku-no-Kagaku* in Japanese). He began sharing his received wisdom by giving lectures, publishing books and monthly magazines of his teachings, and holding seminars for the members of Happy Science.

The ten principles presented in this book are based on lectures Master Okawa gave between 1986 and 1988. Hoping to bring salvation to society as a whole, as well as to each individual, he has now expounded on the essential elements of his teachings and the mission of his movement in this book.

Each year more and more people joined Happy Science to discover and pursue their true potential. Reading *The Science of Happiness* will help you discover extraordinary spiritual Truth and should inspire and awaken you to a higher level of awareness of life and the world. By knowing, understanding, and practicing these Truths, you can certainly find your own path to happiness and enlightenment. Now is the time to embark on your spiritual journey.

PREFACE

A Unique Mission

In June 1981 the spirit of Jesus Christ came down to tell me something extraordinary: I was being called to a unique mission. What Jesus revealed with profound sincerity and love was my calling to be a global spiritual leader to bring salvation and lead humankind to the new future.

When Jesus appeared, my father was there, and he was speechless when he experienced the presence of such a high spirit. When a high spirit makes an appearance on earth in this way, it is with a numinous radiance that causes one's body to become very warm, and the messages communicated are so filled with Truth and light that the overwhelmed recipient's eyes overflow with tears. Such was my experience.

The following month, a hidden part of my consciousness— Shakyamuni Buddha himself—began to speak to me in a mixture of Japanese and Magadhi Prakrit (an ancient Indian language) urging me to embrace my destiny and to spread the word of Buddha. He revealed to me that I am an incarnation of El Cantare,* the supreme consciousness of

---

*El Cantare is the supreme consciousness of this planet Earth who has been guiding humankind from the beginning of life on Earth, and is the great consciousness of the Law that governs all of humankind. A small part of this grand consciousness is sent down to Earth every few thousand years to instruct humankind. Shakyamuni Buddha and Master Okawa are both part of this consciousness. Other reincarnations are: Hermes in Ancient Greece, Rient Arl Cloud of the Incan Empire, Thoth of the Atlantis Empire and La Mu of the Mu Empire.

his group, and that my mission is to save all living creatures through worldwide revelation of the Truth. The role of the Grand Nyorai Shakyamuni is twofold, he advised. There is the dimension represented by the Nyorai Amida (the Savior), which expresses love, compassion, and faith. There is also the dimension represented by the Nyorai Mahavairocana (the essence of the Buddha), which conveys enlightenment, spiritual truth, and secret knowledge of the spiritual domain. If the first aspect were to become dominant within me, I was advised, I would duly become a Grand Savior. But if the second aspect prevailed, I would become the Mahavairocana Buddha (the Great Enlightening).

I was completely taken aback by this information. My upbringing had certainly been religious, and I accepted without question the existence of the spiritual realm. But these revelations were so overpowering, and my designated mission so enormous, that I could not conceal my shocked amazement.

However, I also immediately realized that I am a reincarnation of the Buddha, and that it is my mission to reorganize the high spirits in heaven, while also integrating all the various religions on earth to create a new world religion. It is my responsibility to gather all the people of the world into this new faith, to pioneer the development of a new civilization, and thus to herald the advent of a new age.

However, I did not feel that I was ready to undertake this incredible responsibility, even though I had immediately intuited the authenticity of my calling and accepted it wholeheartedly. Since I was still in my twenties and working for an international trading company, I decided to continue working at my job until I reached the age of thirty. I was, of course, experiencing a great deal of inner turmoil as I functioned in the everyday world of business, while fully aware of my true identity and vocation.

Then, suddenly, my life took another dramatic turn. In 1982 I was assigned as a trainee to my company's headquarters in New York, all the while knowing that I had received a message from Jesus and been commissioned for a cosmic undertaking by the Buddha. Thus, this Buddha-to-be spent many days working with fellow operatives on Wall Street in the intense world of international finance.

Meanwhile, I learned English and studied international finance at the Graduate Center of the City University of New York. I mingled with young businessmen and -women in their early thirties from such companies as Bank of America, Citibank, and Merrill Lynch. Together we learned the ins and outs of the foreign currency exchange system.

But not unexpectedly, I was less than happy in what I was doing. The gap between the mundane realities of my everyday life and the intense experiences of my spirit world grew ever wider. Sometimes I would find myself gazing up at the World Trade Center in lower Manhattan where I worked, and wondering what was truly real: these huge buildings piercing the sky or the voices I could hear in my heart. My sense of identity was severely tested.

The year I spent as a trainee was nonetheless a great success, and my boss asked if he could recommend that I be posted in New York full time. It was an unprecedented opportunity and a clear signal that I was already well on my way to the top of my profession, but I was more interested in compiling into a book the spiritual messages I had been receiving. So, to everyone's astonishment, I turned down the offer and recommended a junior colleague as perfect for the position. People perceived this as an incredible act of selflessness and generosity, rare in business, but I returned to Japan knowing that I had taken a decisive step forward toward my destiny as a religious leader.

I spent the next two years preparing myself for my true mission. In 1985 I began publishing a series of books revealing the spiritual messages I was receiving, including *The Spiritual Message of Jesus Christ*. I was still working for the trading company, so these books were published under my father's name, with my own name appearing only as a contributing writer.

Finally, in June 1986, Jesus and other spirits came to me one after the other and declared that it was time to present myself as the religious leader I'd been commissioned to be. On July 15 of that year—just a week after my thirtieth birthday—I handed in my resignation to the company and felt free to fully embrace my life's mission.

Toward the end of August, I started writing the initial version of *The Laws of the Sun,** completing it in ten days. Shortly thereafter I wrote the companion volume, *The Golden Laws.* These works revealing my message attracted remarkable attention among people sincerely searching for the Truth.

Assembling a Spiritual Community

I gave my first public lecture in Tokyo on March 8, 1987. Some four hundred people turned up to hear me speak on the principles of happiness. In that talk I introduced the four basic principles that constitute the core of what I teach—the principles of love, wisdom, self-reflection, and progress.

That month I also planned the development of the religious movement I had launched. We would dedicate the first three years to study of the basics of the spiritual order, training of religious instructors, and establishment of operational policies as an independent movement. Thereafter, we would concentrate on spreading our message as widely as possible, both nationally and worldwide.

In April 1987, we published the first issue of our monthly magazine, featuring key points of my lectures and other writings, and reporting on the direction and progress of the movement. As I offered further

---

The Laws of the Sun is Ryuho Okawa's best-known work, and one of the most fundamental books that show the structure of the teachings of Happy Science. It illustrates the creation of the Universe, the structure of the spirit world, the development stages of love, the true nature of enlightenment, and the rises and falls of past civilizations from the perspective of El Cantare, the supreme spirit of the terrestrial spirit group. Since it was first published in September 1986, it has become a bestselling title in Japan. *The Laws of the Sun* has also been translated into many languages including English, German, Portuguese, and Korean and has been popular among readers around the world.

lectures and study sessions, the movement grew dramatically, and saw a steady increase in committed members.

My lectures, inspired by my mission and spiritual guidance, captured the hearts and minds of more and more people all over Japan, so attendance at my public talks kept increasing. By 1988, a hall designed to hold two thousand people could not accommodate all who came. In 1989, I spoke to audiences as large as eighty-five hundred, and by 1990, the number swelled to more than ten thousand.

Four years after my initial lecture, on March 7, 1991, Happy Science (Kofuku-no-Kagaku) was officially established as a religious organization. Our new status gave us more credible authority to spread our movement and message into the world. The object of faith is El Cantare, leader of the high spirits of the ninth dimension (about which we reveal more in the course of this book) and reincarnation of the most revered Buddha.

The first annual public celebration of my birthday took place in the Tokyo Dome in July of 1991, with no fewer than fifty thousand believers in attendance. These membership numbers meant that in the same year it was officially established as a religion, Happy Science became one of the largest religious bodies in Japan. The rapid growth of this movement has never been equaled by any other religious group in my country.

In September of that year, we inaugurated an initiative called the Revolution of Hope. Our hope was to free the Japanese people from a prevailing atmosphere of spiritual darkness, and to create an ideal society in postwar Japan.

In 1992 and 1993, I expanded my teachings and clarified the ways in which they are rooted in Buddhist principles. My lectures were broadcast via TV throughout the country, attracting followers all over Japan to the Revolution of Hope campaign, and our total number of believers grew into the millions.

Since those early days, the movement has grown to more than ten million members worldwide. I attribute our success to the significance and timeliness of the mission and message with which I was entrusted.

In this book, I offer in English the spiritual knowledge and wisdom that I have been blessed to receive and commissioned to share with the world.

RYUHO OKAWA

▼

Spiritual dimensions are discussed throughout this book. The table below provides a quick summary of the dimensional structure of the real world and its corresponding realms, spiritual levels, and developmental stages of love. For more detailed descriptions of the dimensions listed below, see the section in chapter 3: The Evolution of Spiritual Awareness.

DIMENSIONAL STRUCTURE OF THE REAL WORLD

Dimensions	Name of Realms	Spiritual Level	Developmental Stages of Love
Ninth	Cosmic Realm	Saviors, Messiahs	Love of Saviors
Eighth	Tathagata Realm	Tathagatas, Great Angels of Light, Great Guiding Spirits of Light	Love Incarnate
Seventh	Bodhisattva Realm	Bodhisattvas, Angels of Light	Forgiving Love
Sixth	Light Realm	Arhats and Angels (upper realm of the sixth dimension)	Spiritually Nurturing Love
Fifth	Realm of the Good		Fundamental Love
Fourth	Posthumous Realm Astral Realm Hell		Instinctive Love
Third	The world on earth		

◄ PART ONE ►

The Dawn of the New Era

It is my fervent wish to have millions of companions who aspire to create an ideal world. In past years, the principle of happiness that I advocate has proved to be the saving path. Based on this evidence, I have launched a great movement for human salvation. I would like to carry this movement forward, hand in hand with those of you who are reading this book. We will work to eradicate atheism and misguided spiritual activities, and establish Truth as the foundational pillar of society. My wish is that more and more people will come to know spiritual Truth and declare the dawn of a new era. You who have taken up this book, awaken! You will play principal roles in the age of salvation.

In the spring of March 1987, at the Ushigome Public Hall in Tokyo, I delivered the first lecture on salvation. With a vow to save humanity, I introduced the principles of happiness, the four major components for achieving happiness: the principles of love, wisdom, self-reflection, and progress. These principles are vitally important and constitute the modern Fourfold Path. It is no exaggeration to say that the development of Happy Science, from that time to the present, was all predicted in that first public lecture. For this reason, I have no hesitation in saying that this book is essential reading for every seeker of the Truth, and that continual study will deepen the seeker's understanding. "The Principle of Love" chapter is offered under the spiritual support of Jesus Christ and predicts the coming of a new era. In "The Principle of the Mind," I've presented a range of ways to explore Right Mind, essential to those who are studying the Truth. I offer this impassioned book to those who have been eagerly anticipating its arrival. This is the time to create an ideal world.

Vow to save humanity, here and now.
Listen, fellow companions,
To the Truth of this message,
If you are caring human beings.

ONE

The Principle of Happiness

Early Adulthood

To begin, I would like to describe how I became involved in the world of religion. I was a university student in my twenties, without much interest in spiritual matters. In those days, however, when I was on a bus or a train, for some reason the word *eternity* would often appear in big white letters before my eyes. I didn't know why the word kept appearing to me, but it happened from time to time. Without any idea of what lay ahead, I would often say to my friends, "In the future I would like to pass on thoughts that will be handed down for thousands of years." I wasn't aware of why I was saying this, but I had a vague dream of becoming a writer, or at least of being a philosopher. Now I understand that, at that time, the stage was already set for my future. But as time passed, my dream started to waver. Although I was attracted to the concept of eternity, and the word *eternity* kept appearing in my mind, I was gradually influenced by my friends, whose aim was to achieve worldly success.

During my student days at the University of Tokyo, I read books on a wide range of subjects, rather than pursuing one field of study. I became interested in the laws that govern society, and unwittingly, I was further drawn to worldly success. Gradually, my wish to get ahead and succeed in the world became stronger and stronger. I thought I would be very happy if, as a result of diligent study, I could dedicate my life to a highly respected job. At that time I had two options: to stay in the academic world and become a scholar, perhaps specializing in political philosophy, or to achieve success outside academia. I continued to waver between these two paths, but as graduation approached and I saw friends start to put their abilities to the test in the larger world, I felt increasingly pulled in that direction. However, I still wanted to study and learn.

I majored in law and studied very diligently. In spite of my efforts, however, my dreams of worldly success were frustrated. At the time, I couldn't figure out why. My classmates seemed to have no trouble finding careers in their chosen fields. Most of the members of my study group succeeded in becoming diplomats and high-ranking public servants, and some entered the legal profession. As graduation neared, my goal was to enter one of these fields after finishing my studies. However, every time I scheduled an exam or job interview, something intervened; it was as if a wall would appear and block my path. I became confused and doubted whether I really should enter the world of business or public affairs.

However, one autumn day I received a phone call from a trading company, and before I knew it, I had accepted their offer. In those days I still wasn't sure what path to take, or in what direction to channel my aspirations. In fact, it's not surprising that I couldn't find a position that matched my ideals, because no profession would have been able to fulfill my yearning for eternity. I had been brought up in a rural area, but ironically, I started to work for a company involved in international trade and was immediately sent to New York City. I found myself in a world completely opposite that of Buddhist or Christian seekers of Truth. It was a dog-eat-dog world where people were chasing numbers, day in and day out.

First thing in the morning, I went to the office a couple of hours before the other employees to read the overseas information sent by Telex (which often amounted to more than thirty feet of paper), analyze it, and consider the day's strategy as quickly as possible. Coffee cup in hand, I scanned the newspapers for the latest economic and financial information, trying to unearth useful clues to trends and critical factors that no one else had yet discovered. That was my work in the trading company.

The Path to the Truth

On March 23, 1981, I quite suddenly began to receive the heavenly revelations that eventually would lead to a decisive turning point in my life.*[1] The first messages, which came from the spirits of the Japanese Buddhist teachers Nikko (1246–1333) and Nichiren (1222–1282),†[2] came as a shock, as if I had been pierced by a shaft of light. The revelation from heaven disclosed that my life was completely on the wrong track. However, I had to hold my life together. After receiving revelations from the heavenly world, I felt I would not be able to continue living an ordinary life. Yet it was impossible to live on alms, as monks used to do, so I sought somehow to balance my business career and my quest for eternal Truth. Over the next four or five years I continued seeking the Truth while still working in the company. But my spiritual seeking occupied less than ten percent of my time. At that point, although I was continuously receiving spiritual messages, I was still uncertain as to what lay ahead, so I decided not to make any dramatic changes in my life until I had a clear vision of my future course. In any case, I was young and not experienced enough to communicate my extraordinary discoveries to other people.

---

*At the first revelation, the words "Good News" repeatedly came through in automatic writing.

†Nichiren, founder of the Nichiren sect of Buddhism in the thirteenth century, taught devotion to the Lotus Sutra. Nichiren Buddhists believe that enlightenment can be attained in the present lifetime.

I thought, "The spiritual phenomena that I am experiencing must be real, but if I start to teach people now, I will surely fail. People will think I'm out of my mind. For now, I just need to be patient and constantly strive to learn, so as to compensate for my lack of experience." So I decided to wait patiently until I gained the confidence to teach people the Truth that was being revealed to me. I thought I should wait until the time was ripe, believing that before long the moment would surely come to make a move.

I continued to accumulate many kinds of spiritual experiences. Finally, after returning to Japan (having turned down a significant promotion in New York), eventually giving up the business world and undertaking a prolonged retreat, I published a number of books of spiritual messages, and was amazed that they became bestsellers in Japan. But I had also received hundreds of other communications that I didn't publish at that time. I have had contact with hundreds of high spirits.* For my first book, *The Spiritual Messages of Nichiren,* I spent four years accumulating data, which means that in addition to what appeared in that book, there were one hundred times that number of additional messages. Hence, that book had a remarkably solid foundation of experience and received wisdom. I was determined that without such a foundation, I would not make any move forward. I also realized that Nichiren was only an initial guide, and that beyond him were four or five hundred high spirits who were ready to support me.

Three or four months after my first spiritual communications, I started to receive messages from Jesus Christ. However, instead of conveying these messages immediately, I spent some time confirming their authenticity. In fact it was at least another three years before I finally comfirmed that the messages from Nichiren were genuine.

---

*The high spirits are those who reside in the upper realms of the sixth dimension and above in the spirit world. They include angels of light, as well as those who are preparing to become angels of light.

The Responsibility of a Religious Leader

There are many newly established religious organizations in these tumultuous times, and most of the leaders of these groups started preaching as soon as they had unusual spiritual experiences. However, many do not seem to realize how great a religious leader's responsibility is. A simple mistake can mislead millions of people, not only in this age, but also in future generations. Such damage cannot be corrected easily.

Spiritual contact with many deceased religious leaders has led me to be extremely cautious, which is why I refrained from taking action until I could confirm with certainty the authenticity of the revelations I'd received from Nichiren. For more than four years his messages were coherent and his character was consistent. The messages were so logical and inspiring that the smartest people on earth could not hope to equal them.

On the other hand, spirits from hell are inconsistent. No matter how fervent their efforts, the inconsistencies in what they say are soon revealed. Ordinary damned spirits are straightforward; they only complain of their pain. However, Satan and his demons* are very experienced and quite shrewd. They boast of their religious knowledge regarding, for example, karma,† or reincarnation.‡ They may even send messages, such as, "Save people. I'm conveying God's words to you, so you must spread these messages to the people. Publish my messages as a book and deliver it to each and every house." Even if you hear them say things like this, you need to be cautious. Spiritual intelligence, or knowledge of the Truth, is essential in order to unearth these spirits' real intentions.

---

*Satan and his demons are spirits in the deepest part of hell who cannot reflect on their thoughts and deeds, and continue committing evil deeds even after death. A number of them were religious leaders or politicians who misled many people while they were alive.

†Karma comprises of soul tendencies developed during past incarnations, and which affect our present life.

‡Reincarnation is the law that every human soul is given eternal life, and is repeatedly reborn on earth in order to refine the soul.

There may be malicious spirits who have strong psychic powers or will-power, but they do not have a systematic knowledge of universal Truth, because there is no place in hell to learn such truths.

However, if you humbly study not only Buddhism but also a variety of religions, such as Christianity, Shintoism, and Taoism; and if you study morality, philosophy, and science as well, your deepened under-standing enables you to grasp the golden thread that runs through all thought and science, and recognize the inconsistencies in what demons say. In contrast, those who believe exclusively in, for example, esoteric Buddhism or a particular sect of Christianity, keeping their eyes shut tight against other ideas, can easily be deluded by a malicious spirit, one who is an expert in that particular belief. You may come across these sorts of believers in certain Christian sects. I myself have been accosted by such people.

One day, when I came out of a subway station, a woman from a Christian sect approached me and asked, "Could you spare me a moment?" She didn't give me a chance to refuse, but continued, "You seem to be in trouble." Of course I was in trouble, wondering how I could escape from her. She went on, "Perhaps you are possessed by some bad spirit. I can purify you if you can spare a couple of minutes." I declined to be purified on the street. Then she said, "Why don't we move somewhere quieter?" I did my best to refuse her offer. But she was relentless, insisting that she had to save as many lambs as possible. Finally, I was forced to make an excuse in order to escape.

Having observed new religions and seen their founders in the after-life, I strongly resolved not to undertake the path of religion unless I could do so with total conviction. Normally, no one would wait six years after receiving messages from Nichiren or Jesus Christ. Usually people who have such experiences start spreading the word immediately, but I did not. I decided that even if it took years, I wouldn't take any steps to appear in public until I could positively confirm that the spiritual mes-sages I'd received really were from high spirits. Happy Science has been prudent and careful in its activities.

I started out very modestly, wanting to build a firm foundation before presenting my own teachings. My books of spiritual messages represent only a tiny portion of all the knowledge I have acquired. They are selected messages that I have analyzed and confirmed to be true. Those who join Happy Science are required to cultivate Right Mind daily, but some quickly forget this necessity, even if they were inspired at the beginning. However, for years I have continued cultivating Right Mind daily. Otherwise it is impossible to communicate with high spirits. You must attain the same vibration as high spirits if you want to communicate with them. This is the law of the universe, and there are no exceptions.

What Is a Prophet?

Prophets are different from ordinary spiritual mediums. While mediums hear the words of the spirits of ordinary people who have passed away, prophets can hear the words of high spirits. They do not simply predict what is going to happen; they convey the words and will of God.

One example is Moses, who led the Israelites out of slavery in Egypt thousands of years ago. Moses could hear the voices of divine spirits of the ninth dimension because he was a prophet. It was his mission to convey the words of these divine spirits.

Another prophet, Elijah, who lived nearly three thousand years ago, challenged five hundred priests of Baal in order to show them the error of their belief that Baal would grant people whatever they wished for. Their worship of the storm-god Baal, also known as the god of fertility, had been unable to reverse the drought prophesied by Elijah. The prophet said, "You call on the name of your god, and I will call on the name of the Lord. The god who answers by fire—he is God" (1 Kings 18:24).

The Mount Carmel confrontation started early in the morning. The pagan priests laid a sacrifice on the altar and prayed to Baal to ignite it. From morning till noon they prayed to their god, but there was no answer, no fire from heaven. Midday passed and they began to slash themselves with swords and spears, as was their custom. Covered in blood, they danced and continued praying aloud, but still no fire appeared. On seeing this, Elijah began to mock and taunt them. He called out to his god, Yahweh, and no sooner did he begin praying than a fire from heaven roared down, setting his altar ablaze and consuming his sacrifice. Shortly thereafter, rain fell for the first time in three years. (See chapter 5 of *The Golden Laws.*)

More recently, Jesus Christ was sent from heaven. When Jesus was asked by one of his disciples, "Lord, show us the Father and that will be enough for us" (John 14:8), he answered, "Don't you believe that I am in the Father, and that the Father is in me? The words I say to you are not just my own. Rather, it is the Father, living in me, who is doing his work" (John 14:10). The truth was that great divine spirits came down and spoke through Jesus. Divine spirits of the ninth dimension preached through Jesus, or, rather, they inspired him when he preached. That is why Jesus used to say, "Believe me when I say that I am in the Father and the Father is in me" (John 14:11). Jesus was conveying the words of these divine spirits.

Mohammed (570–632 CE) was a trader and desert camel driver who became a prophet. At the age of forty, while meditating in a cave, Mohammed heard a loud voice say to him, "Mohammed, I am the god, Allah." Although initially frightened, Mohammed came to realize the significance of this spiritual experience. He received numerous revelations from heaven, and these divine messages are the basis of the Koran, the teachings of Islam. Mohammed listened attentively and memorized the messages and later repeated them to his followers, who scribed them on parchment, bones, or whatever was handy. (See chapter 5 of *The Golden Laws.*)

Thus, throughout history, divine spirits have come to Earth as prophets to convey God's words.

First Learn, Then Teach

At Happy Science we place great importance on knowledge, because without it, one cannot distinguish right from wrong. This is not the sort of knowledge needed for school exams, but knowledge of spiritual Truth. If you examine existing religious teachings and philosophies against the knowledge of the Truth found in our books, you will find some inconsistencies. In other words, our books contain certain tacit criticisms.

Knowledge, as we know, is power. So for the first step, I would like you to acquire knowledge of the Truth, for knowledge is very important. When you read the books of the Truth, please don't be satisfied with reading a book just once; check and see whether you have really assimilated what you've read.

If you want to deepen your academic studies, there are many teachers, but there is nowhere to check whether or not your understanding of the Truth is correct. Our intention is to convey the Truth throughout the world, but at the present time, I place the utmost importance on making our foundation solid. Our basic strategy is first strengthening the inside, then the outside; building the foundation and then the pillars. The correct order is exploring the Truth, studying it, and conveying it to others.

Just as I spent six years creating the foundations of Happy Science, first study the Truth thoroughly. Consider carefully what you want to convey. As Jesus Christ said, "If a blind man leads a blind man, both will fall into a pit" (Matthew 15:14). You cannot teach others what you don't understand. New religions often create problems, because those who have not yet attained true spiritual wisdom try to lead other people and draw them into their organization. It's wonderful to talk with someone who has a good personality, possesses vast spiritual knowledge, and has an understanding of the Truth. But usually this is not the case, so followers try to convert others to their religion by force, making everyone feel uncomfortable.

To avoid similar problems, it's better to spend some time exploring the Truth and studying it before we convey it to others. This is why I kept our organization to a study group for the first couple of years. We did not yet have any lecturers to teach newcomers, and an expansion of membership at that stage would only have given rise to confusion. So in the first few years, I cultivated people who had enough knowledge of the Truth, lecturers who could teach others and who would become the core of our missionary effort. Now, I have built the foundations for teaching the Laws, so before you think of teaching anything, first please study. To explain what I am saying now in Buddhist terms, Mahayana can only start after Theravada has been established.* Only after you have attained enlightenment can you save others. When people start doing the reverse of what I am saying, there can be tragic consequences. So first find happiness for yourself before trying to make others happy.

Happy Science started its activities as a kind of Theravada group. But now, I would like to disseminate the Truth all over the world with the inner foundations firmly established. What did you learn from the teachings of Happy Science? Unless you can answer this question, you cannot teach people the Truth.

The Fourfold Path to True Happiness

Finally, I would like to address the main theme of this lecture, the principles of happiness, which are unique to Happy Science. There are numerous ways to become happy, but the kind of happiness I am talking about is not the sort you can enjoy only in this world. It is a joy that carries over from this world to the next. We're exploring principles of happiness that apply to the past, the present, and the future.

---

*In Buddhism, the more traditional Theravada school adheres precisely to meditation and Shakyamuni Buddha's teachings in the pursuit of higher enlightenment. The Mahayana movement, or "movement for the masses," reformulated Buddha's teachings with the intention of saving as many people as possible.

The starting point of these principles is willingness to explore Right Mind. Every individual has a diamond within, and this pure diamond represents Right Mind. You may think that highly developed spirits are better than lower-level spirits, for example, that Tathagatas* of the eighth dimension are greater than Bodhisattvas of the seventh, and Bodhisattvas† are better than the spirits in the Light Realm of the sixth dimension in the other world.

However, people should not be judged by their spiritual level alone. The diamond within everyone is essentially the same, the only difference being in the level of refinement and the brilliance of the diamond, which is the result of numerous incarnations. Those who make the effort to polish the diamond within become angels of light. So if you continue to refine your inner diamond, it will surely shine. This is true for everyone.

However, no one can become a Tathagata instantly. To make your diamond shine brightly, you must put forth constant and tireless efforts. These efforts are exactly the same as the exploration of Right Mind; this is the spiritual discipline that allows you to discover your true nature. Through daily effort to explore Right Mind, you will enter the next stage, in which you seek true happiness.

Love

The first principle of happiness is love. This love is not the kind of love that you expect to receive from others. The love that I teach at Happy Science is love that gives.[3] The true nature of love that gives is based on awakening to the fact that all human beings are children of God and originate in him, and that you are essentially one with others. Even if

---

*A Tathagata (Sanskrit and Pali) is a Great Guiding Spirit of Light who resides in the eighth dimension of the Real World. A Tathagata is an embodiment of the Absolute Truth, a being who manifests love toward humans and instructs us. The term implies a transcendence of the human condition.

†A Bodhisattva (Sanskrit) is an angel of light who resides in the seventh dimension of the Real World. A Bodhisattva is motivated by compassion and is dedicated to enlightening and saving people through the will of Buddha.

you seem to have a completely different personality from anyone around you, your true nature is essentially the same as the true nature of everyone else. This is the basis of true love. It is only because you think you are separate from other people that friction and discord arise. Once we have awakened to the fact that essentially we are all one, that we all originate from God and are all his children, we naturally come to love one another. We may have different personalities, but each of us is expected to realize our common spiritual essence while valuing our individuality.

What exactly does it mean to love others? It means wishing for the good of others, and wishing to nurture others without expecting anything in return. It is a selfless love, detached from personal desire. Because your essence and the essence of others is the same, you are required to love others just as you love yourself. It is easy to love ourselves; it's not something we need to be taught. But unfortunately, once we have been born into a physical body and experience ourselves as separate and distinct, we forget to love others. This is why we need to learn to practice love that gives.

The teaching of love sounds very Christian, but love that gives is the same as compassion, which is the basis of Shakyamuni Buddha's teachings. Translated into modern terms, Shakyamuni taught, "First, think of giving love." This was the meaning of his teachings on compassion. Love, therefore, is the first principle of happiness.

Wisdom

The second principle of happiness is wisdom. As I mentioned before, it is important to have a correct knowledge of spiritual Truth. Without this knowledge of Truth, human beings cannot be free in the truest sense. I feel truly free because I am confident in my correct knowledge of the Truth. Some religions don't understand this concept. Take, for example, Christian missionaries who come to Japan. In their zeal to convert and save people, they insist, "You must throw away your Buddhist altar and convert to Christianity. You cannot enter heaven unless you abandon

Buddhism." These missionaries may be pure in heart and dedicated, but they are unaware of the Truth. They believe that unless people abandon their faith in "heretical" Buddhism, they cannot go to heaven. They feel relieved to see people converting to Christianity, confident that they now will be able to enter heaven.

High spirits in heaven feel unhappy when they see this. Many dedicated religious people believe that only their particular brand of religion can save people, because they don't know that Truth can also be found in other religions. Such confusion is very sad. To avoid this, you need to have correct knowledge of the Truth. This is the real meaning of the phrase "The Truth will set you free" (John 8:32).

Self-Reflection

The third principle of happiness is self-reflection, which is closely related to the cultivation of Right Mind. We are essentially all children of God with brilliantly shining souls. However, just as a diamond accumulates dirt if it is neglected, our souls inevitably collect dust and grime as we live in this world. Our life mission is to refine the soul.

Of course, there may be help from an outside power; it's like getting help from a specialist, and sometimes we need that help. But instead of doing nothing while waiting for help, we need to get busy polishing our own diamond. If we do not refine ourselves, what is the meaning of practicing spirituality?

During the course of your life, mistakes sometimes occur. If you realize you've made a mistake, who can correct it except you? Although someone else could wash your body, only you can cleanse your soul. Self-Reflection is based on personal power;* it helps us to see what needs to be polished. Start by reflecting on your past thoughts and deeds. There's no point in gold plating rusty metal. If there is rust beneath, the shiny surface will soon peel away.

---

*Teachings about the power of personal power are based on the spirit of self-help. It is the attitude of actively accepting the challenge of spiritual refinement and improving oneself through one's own efforts.

The teaching of self-reflection is the path to the level of Arhat,* the upper realm of the sixth dimension. Arhat is the preparatory stage for becoming an angel of light, a Bodhisattva. Before entering this gateway to the level of Bodhisattva, it is essential to follow the path of self-reflection. You must endeavor to remove the "rust" from your mind, allowing a spiritual aura, or halo, to emanate from you. Aim first for the level of Arhat, a level we all can reach in this lifetime. Although everyone has accumulated karma, or rust on the soul from past incarnations, and although we are all going through different stages of spiritual development, everyone—without exception—can attain the level of Arhat. It is much more difficult to advance to the stages beyond this, but through spiritual refinement you will certainly be able to develop a spiritual aura and become an Arhat. This is the true purpose of practicing self-reflection. If we produce one thousand Arhats in every country, their work as politicians, teachers, and business leaders will exert a great influence on the people around them, and society will eventually change. One Arhat can influence fifty or even a hundred people, so if there are one thousand Arhats, about one hundred thousand people will gradually change, and those one hundred thousand will change another million, and so on. I believe this is the right way to spread the Truth.

Progress

Self-reflection precedes the fourth principle of happiness: progress. If people seek progress without the practice of self-reflection, they will most likely face difficulties before they attain success. One can become an Arhat when one reaches a certain level of enlightenment. When people reach the next level of practicing loving and saving others, they advance to the level of Bodhisattva of the seventh dimension.

---

*Arhat is the state that corresponds to the upper realm of the sixth dimension. Here one has removed the clouds that cover the mind by practicing self-reflection, and is undergoing spiritual refinement to attain the state of Bodhisattva. (See chapter 4 of *The Laws of the Sun*.)

Bodhisattvas then proceed to the Tathagata Realm, where there is no darkness, no evil or shadow, only light.

These steps clearly show that the dualism of good and evil does not conflict with the idea that only light exists. (See chapter 2 of *The Laws of the Sun.*) It is simply a question of different stages. Most people first need to practice self-reflection in the world of duality, and once they have finished cleansing their souls, they can enter the world where only light exists. It is an undeniable fact that there are distinct levels in the spirit world,* and one must progress from one stage to the next. The spirits in the fourth dimension cannot leap straight to the eighth dimension; they first need to attain mastery of the fifth dimension. The spirits in the fifth dimension must first aim to go to the sixth dimension, then to the Bodhisattva Realm of the seventh, then to the Tathagata Realm of the eighth dimension. This is how progress can be achieved on the path of self-reflection; without the feeling of making progress, you cannot feel truly happy.

The last principle of happiness is progress: the development of the self, of others, and of society. The ultimate goal is to create a utopia, an ideal world on earth. The four principles of happiness, then, are love, wisdom, self-reflection, and progress. This is the modern Fourfold Path that will lead you to true happiness. This is the first gateway to the Theravada path that I teach. There will be further steps, but as the first step, I would like you to explore the Fourfold Path of love, wisdom, self-reflection, and progress. I'm sure that you will develop your own unique, true happiness.

---

*The spirit world is clearly divided into many dimensions, and these correspond to one's spiritual vibrations and state of mind; therefore, each spirit goes to the corresponding realm.

TWO

The Principle of Love

The Laws of the Sun through the Passage of Time

In ages past, there was an enormous continent located to the south of Japan, centered on what is now Jakarta, Indonesia. The continent was called Mu, and there the Mu Empire flourished until the continent sank into the ocean without a trace, about fifteen thousand years ago. Two thousand years earlier, the great emperor La Mu, or the Light of Mu, was born there. During the seventy-three years of his life, he taught the Laws of the Sun, and the Mu Empire enjoyed the last of its prosperity.

Next, La Mu incarnated in Atlantis as Thoth, about twelve thousand years ago. Atlantis was a great empire with a highly advanced scientific technology that, in some ways, surpassed even that of today. As I indicated in *The Laws of the Sun,* at that time the Atlanteans already possessed airships. They were whale-shaped, and more than ninety-eight feet long. On top of these airships were pyramids that looked like dorsal fins, which converted solar energy into power to turn the tail propellers; underneath was the passenger compartment. The airships were kept afloat with gas, but since they were powered by solar energy, they were unable to fly on cloudy or rainy days.

Solar energy was also used for ocean transportation. There were orca-shaped vessels that resembled present-day submarines. In place of the dorsal fin, there were three pyramids. Because these vessels operated on solar energy, they occasionally had to surface to absorb sunlight and recharge their solar pyramids.

Atlantis had an early form of democracy and well-rounded politicians. Most of the people in government were also religious leaders and scientists. Thoth's genius extended to many fields, including religion, politics, and science. The main teachings of Thoth, however, were the principle of love and the principle of wisdom, which included the structure of the universe. Both teachings appear in chapter 5 of *The Laws of the Sun*.

Thoth next incarnated, about seven thousand years ago, as Rient Arl Croud, into the ancient kingdom of the Inca in the Andes mountains of Peru. There his teachings focused on how to restore the human mind to its original state.

You may have visited the Andes or seen aerial photographs of the strange geometric figures on TV or in magazines. These patterns, recognizable only from the sky, look like runways, or some kind of message. There is also a design of a human figure with an arm upraised. These figures suggest watchers from above—not earthly beings, but beings from space. The notion of visitors from space is popular nowadays, but, in fact, many extraterrestrials have visited our planet.

The Inca worshipped the visitors as gods. However, Rient Arl Croud admonished them, explaining that the visitors were only strangers who were more scientifically advanced. He said that people from these civilizations shouldn't be regarded as gods simply because of their technological achievements. He taught, "God is not something that exists outside you; he dwells within. Try to find God within yourself." At a time when people's minds were directed outward, Rient Arl Croud taught them to look inward.

Later, about 4,200 years ago, Rient Arl Croud incarnated in Greece as Hermes. While most people know Hermes as one of the

Greek gods, he actually lived several hundred years prior to Zeus.*

The central theme of his teaching was prosperity, which is still being handed down as the Laws of Prosperity, and corresponds to the principle of progress that I teach. As Hermes' teachings of prosperity spread, arts and literature flourished throughout Greece. Thus, preparations were made for Zeus and Apollo to be born in the flesh and become active in the arts.

During Hermes' lifetime the Greeks enjoyed peace and wealth while practicing the Truth correctly. But as time passed, they began to misinterpret the teachings and became corrupt; from prosperity they strayed to decadence. Watching this from heaven, Hermes resolved to teach a quite opposite philosophy in his next incarnation, one that would deliver souls from worldly attachment.

Hermes then incarnated in India 2,600 years ago, this time as the well-known Gautama Siddhartha, Shakyamuni Buddha. He taught that true happiness is found not in the pursuit of worldly desires, but in eliminating attachment. He also taught that everyone has a kingdom within, a kingdom that no one else can invade. Even without money, social status, or fame, this kingdom is of great value. That is why Gautama, born a prince and living in a palace until he was twenty-nine years old, renounced a life of luxury and set out as a mendicant.

He thought, "The fame and status that I have had for twenty-nine years are meaningless. I started from nothing when I was born into this world, and now I will start over again from zero." For six years he followed ascetic practices as he meditated and sought enlightenment. Finally, about three months prior to his thirty-sixth birthday, he attained his great enlightenment beneath a pipal, or bodhi tree, the nature of which I reveal in my discussion of the principle of enlightenment.

---

*The stories of Greek gods changed as they were handed down through the ages in the form of Greek myths; only 10 to 20 percent of them are accurate. In fact, Hermes lived around 2300 BCE and founded the Greek civilization, which was to become the basis of Western civilization. Hermes is the god of prosperity and the arts; he guided the people of Hellenistic Egypt under the name Hermes Trismegistus, and was also known as Thoth.

So the spirit of La Mu eventually reincarnated as Hermes, who taught prosperity and development; and was then reborn as Shakyamuni Buddha, whose teachings centered on self-reflection. This was the progress of La Mu's Laws of the Sun through sixteen thousand years. Now I am following the same path—the Fourfold Path, also called the principles of happiness—which consists of love, wisdom, self-reflection, and progress. This path integrates Hermes' teachings of love and progress and Shakyamuni Buddha's teachings of wisdom and self-reflection. I set down these two types of teachings as the foundation of my activities. This is the historical background of my foundational book of teachings, *The Laws of the Sun.*

The Prophecy of Salvation

The publication of my foundational book, *The Laws of the Sun,* was predicted more than four hundred years ago in France by Michel de Nostredame (Nostradamus). His book, *Centuries,* is a collection of symbolic predictions in poetry. These predictions were not specific, but hinted at what may happen in the future, although his specific predictions do not go beyond the year 2000. He predicted a significant event in July of 1999, and hinted that this event could signify the end of humankind. However, the esoteric poems also say that if the world continues as it is, it may end in the twenty-first century. But there is still hope. Hermes will reappear in the East, says Nostradamus, and the success of Hermes can save humankind. In another section, Nostradamus writes that the Laws of the Sun will be taught in the East, descendants of angels will be born to save the world, and a new Golden Age will begin in plain sight.

In my book *The Golden Laws,* I detail the history of the angels of light in the West, the East, and Japan specifically, as well as how the future of humanity will unfold. I explain that the Golden Age will surely come.* I am not the only one who was born to create this Golden

---

*As Nostradamus predicted, the Laws of the Sun were taught in the East, and as a result, his predictions of world war and invasion by a "king of terror" in 1999 were averted. (With regard to the future of humanity, see chapter 6 of *The Golden Laws.*)

Age. All of you who are reading this book were born to create this Golden Age. You have come across my book because you have listened to my voice many times before, through tens of thousands of years. Just as you study my words today, you have studied my words before. The energy of one or two people is not enough to create the Golden Age; to open up this future we must join hands and initiate a powerful surge of divine energy.

We were born into this world to begin this movement, and many angels of light will join us. I did not start Happy Science to form a single religious group. Hundreds of religious leaders are already claiming to be Messiahs and forming groups, and I don't intend to compete with them. I came to this world to integrate all the different teachings that are derived from one and the same source, and to build the foundation of the Golden Age. Though the first phase of our movement may seem to be a religious reformation, it is not my intention to destroy or confuse other religious groups by claiming that only my teachings are right.

The first stage of our movement will bring about dramatic changes in the world of religion. This is not, however, our final goal. In the second stage, our movement will bring radical change throughout the whole of society. Just as many people have risen to build the foundation of nations throughout history, many "warriors of light" will start their work to create utopia, and will reform everything in a fundamental way: politics, economics, education, the arts, literature, and business. Academic studies will be restructured, the modern worldly values that make religion incompatible with politics will be reversed, and the Truth will be restored to its rightful place as central to all other values.

This world is God's creation, so those who govern a country or this world must be God's envoys and act on his behalf; they should not govern people simply using political skills or on the basis of popularity. Unless those who understand the Truth guide and govern the people, how is it possible to realize an ideal world on earth?

Then this movement will enter the third stage. In this stage our books will be translated into many languages and published worldwide, but it will not be merely the expansion of a single school of religious thought. Rather, the revolution to create utopia on earth will spread across the whole world.

When Shakyamuni Buddha taught the Truth in India, his teaching did not extend beyond India because of the limitations of his time. He anticipated that his teachings would spread to China and Japan some day, but that expectation was not realized in his lifetime.

Jesus Christ faced similar obstacles. Two thousand years ago Jesus was born to save the world, but again, he was subject to the limitations of his time. While he preached mainly in Palestine, there were many countries and races in his era that had their own cultures, political views and practices, and religious beliefs, and either never heard Jesus's teachings or considered them alien. Although Jesus's teachings were powerful, how many people did they reach? How many heard his famous Sermon on the Mount? No matter how compelling his words, perhaps only a few thousand people were able to experience and hear him. As I've learned in the messages I have received, only a portion of his teachings was passed on in the Gospels.

Now we live in very fortunate circumstances. Every time I give a lecture, my words are recorded and spread not only across Japan, but also across the world. They are also being preserved for the people of the future.

The Love of Jesus

Two thousand years ago, Jesus Christ started his great work after he was baptized at the age of thirty by John the Baptist. Soon after he began, twelve apostles gathered around Jesus to help him. They remembered his words and deeds, and spread his message to different places. When Jesus was nearly thirty-three years old, a young man who was not yet twenty accompanied Jesus everywhere he went, earnestly studying his teachings and memorizing them. The young man's name was Mark, and he was the author of the first Gospel.*

Great guiding spirits of light have descended to earth and taught the Law through different ages, but the most difficult problem has always been how to convey the Law to everyone. Jesus eloquently revealed many vital truths during his three years of missionary activities, but unfortunately, less than one percent of what he said was recorded and remains in the New Testament today.

While he lived on earth, Jesus was guided by many different spirits,† and I, the El Cantare consciousness, was his main guiding spirit.‡ I know the discipline Jesus followed from his birth until the age of thirty, as well as his thoughts and teachings from then until he was crucified three years later. It is because I, as the El Cantare consciousness, was guiding him from heaven at that time. Now I often communicate with him spiritually, just as two thousand years ago I, as the El Cantare consciousness, communicated with him to suggest ways of conveying the Truth.

Jesus often prayed. Early in the morning, while people were still sleeping, Jesus would go to the Mount of Olives, kneel, and pray to heaven. At that time I, El Cantare, communicated to him about ways of conveying the Truth and the different stages of love. There were other spirits who sent him spiritual messages; among them were Elijah and Michael.

---

*According to my spiritual research, Mark is an actual figure who lived in the same age as Jesus and was indeed the author of the Gospel of Mark. His reincarnation, my father Saburo Yoshikawa, helped with the recording, transcribing, editing, and publishing of spiritual messages received from high spirits from 1981 to 1986. He later served as honorary adviser to Happy Science.

†When a prophet descends to earth to start a religious movement, s/he is guided by a group of high spirits in heaven. However they tend to use one name or "one-window" so that people in this world do not get confused in having faith in a certain religion. Similarly, Jesus Christ was guided by different angels and high spirits in heaven when he was on earth.

‡The El Cantare consciousness is the supreme being of the terrestrial spirit group. For more information about the El Cantare consciousness, see *The Laws of the Sun*.

Buddhism teaches stages of enlightenment, and although Christians today may be unfamiliar with this idea, there are also stages of love.

Christianity and Buddhism went separate ways because this philosophy was not spread widely enough. Jesus tried to follow the spiritual guidance I gave him from heaven, "There are stages of love, and human beings need to go through these stages in order to progress and become more enlightened." But the people who gathered around Jesus were not spiritually mature enough to understand the stages of love. Even the twelve apostles were no exception. Although they were close to Jesus, they had difficulty understanding the stages of love in the journey toward enlightenment. Unlike the scribes and the priests, most of the disciples were fishermen who had not studied the Law. Literacy and education were very limited in those times, as was the amount of scripture one could hear in the synagogue.

Originally Jesus had planned to guide people step-by-step, but unexpected difficulties blocked his way in the form of religious persecution. The scribes and priests, who took Jesus's teachings to be wrong, accused him of being a false prophet.

The scribes were specialists in the study of the laws God gave to Moses on Mount Sinai more than three thousand years ago, and the priests were experts in rituals and purity laws. They followed every word of the laws of Moses to the letter, focusing on the details of what Moses had said, constantly arguing over their interpretation. They did not understand that Moses was also subject to the constraints of his time, and insisted that there could be no modifications in Moses's teachings. For instance, he had said, "Observe the Sabbath day by keeping it holy, as the Lord your God has commanded you" (Deuteronomy 5:12), and hence the scribes and priests held rigidly to the rule of not working in any way on the Sabbath.

The truth is, however, that the Sabbath is an expression of God's compassion. God commanded human beings to work six days a week. He did not say simply to rest on the seventh day, but rather he asked people to use the last day of the week for devotion to him. He meant that on busy working days, people do not have time to sit quietly, face-to-face with God, so it is important to set aside one day a week to calm the heart and mind. A holiday was originally a "holy day," a day set aside as sacred.

Seeing Jesus's teachings spreading like wildfire throughout Palestine, the religious leaders felt threatened. They feared that unless they took action, their authority would be jeopardized and that Jesus might oust them from their positions. Just as the Brahmins* had persecuted Shakyamuni in India five hundred years earlier, they accused and condemned Jesus, and ultimately demanded his life.

At every opportunity the authorities laid traps to snare Jesus.

They brought a sick man to Jesus on the Sabbath and watched what he would do. Jesus, of course, did not leave the sick man waiting until the following day. Jesus asked the sick man, "Do you believe in me?" When the sick man answered, "Lord, I believe," Jesus said to him, "Be as you believe yourself to be." He meant, "If you believe that you are a child of God, then rise as a child of God would." The sick man became well and rose from his bed. It was not Jesus who had healed him; the man awakened to his original state as a perfect child of God when Jesus reminded him of his true nature.

On witnessing this scene the scribes accused Jesus, saying, "You broke God's commandment not to work on the Sabbath. You healed a sick person." Jesus replied, "Do you think God has ever taken a rest for even one day since he divided this universe into heaven and earth? If God rested, even for a day, how could all of creation continue to live? Has the sun ever stopped giving out heat and light to us, for even a single day? Like the sun, God has never ceased working since the day of creation. Then why am I, as a child of God, prohibited from healing a sick person on the Sabbath? If a lamb fell into a pit on the Sabbath, would the shepherd wait till the next day to rescue it? He would surely help the lamb right away. It should not matter if it is the Sabbath if one can save the eternal life of a human being, a child of

*Brahmin is the priestly class in India, the highest of the four main castes.

God, the being closest to God. You are mistaken in your beliefs."*

Jesus spoke the Truth, but the sharpness of his challenge created many enemies, who feared change even if it was for the good. So I, as the El Cantare consciousness, said to Jesus, "Be patient and teach the Truth step-by-step. People cannot become enlightened instantly, so do not be hasty. You need to start educating people in stages; otherwise your life will not last more than three years." But Jesus replied, "I would not regret losing my life. I cannot rest, even for a day, even for a moment. When the children of God are suffering so much, how can I rest and not take any action to remove their suffering? No doctor would leave a patient bleeding with a thorn stuck in his flesh, and no teacher would not offer a helping hand to a student who was failing."

Jesus chose to save the lives of many rather than just his own. His original plan was to teach the different levels of love and lead people to enlightenment, but as enemies appeared, maintaining good relations with his persecutors became his main concern. His daily life was a severe ordeal, for he was constantly exposed to danger.

You may remember his words in the Bible: "Foxes have holes and birds of the air have nests, but the Son of Man has no place to lay his head" (Matthew 8:20). Day after day Jesus fled, moving from house to house where people hid him. He couldn't risk openly building a solid foundation for his teachings on love, as had been originally planned.

Because his disciples were ready to fight his enemies, Jesus had no choice but to teach mainly of the love that negates evil. He said, "Love your enemies and pray for those who try to persecute you. If you pray for those who love you, what credit is that to you? Even the pagans do this. Those who have studied my teachings should pray for the people who try to persecute and kill them, rather than for those who support them." Thus, forgiveness became the core of his teachings.

---

*This preaching of Jesus is described in the Bible as follows: "He said to them, 'If any of you has a sheep and it falls into a pit on the Sabbath, will you not take hold of it and lift it out? How much more valuable is a man than a sheep! Therefore it is lawful to do good on the Sabbath'" (Matthew 12:11–12).

Jesus taught about love by dividing it into two different types: "Love your neighbor as yourself" and "Love the Lord your God." He taught that loving one's neighbors is important, saying, "Loving your family is not so difficult. Look at animals; they cherish their young. If animals can do this, why is it such an effort for you? It is important that you love your father and mother, your son and daughter, but as human beings, it is only natural to love your own family." Jesus taught that we should love all those we chance to meet in our lives, our "neighbors." He also taught a higher love, the love for God. He said, "Love the Lord your God with all your heart and with all your soul and with all your mind" (Matthew 22:37). Jesus taught people to love others and to love God, but before he could teach the next stage, his life was cut short.

This is why heaven sent St. Bernard to Europe in the eleventh century.* He was in reality a reincarnation of Nagarjuna of India, who spread the teachings of Mahayana Buddhism.† St. Bernard explained the different stages of love, teaching that supreme love serves others on God's behalf, but his teachings were incomplete. Even a great saint like St. Bernard could not explain the stages of love in as logical a way as Buddhism explains enlightenment.

Jesus Christ's teachings of love and Shakyamuni Buddha's teachings of enlightenment are both from the same source, so there should be no essential contradiction between the two. However, those who teach "personal power" emphasize the stages of enlightenment, while those who give preeminence to an outside power focus on the idea of loving all equally, as extensions of one another and of that higher power.

Thus, Buddhism emphasizes the various stages of enlightenment, while Christianity emphasizes equal love for all. Because of the difference in their focus and direction, most Buddhists and Christians find mutual understanding difficult, believing they have little in common.

---

*St. Bernard of Clairvaux (1090–1153) was a French theologian and Christian mystic. He is the author of *On Loving God*.

†Nagarjuna, who was born in the second century CE, is said to be the founder of the Madhyamika school of Mahayana Buddhism. (Refer to chapter 3 of *The Golden Laws*.)

Shakyamuni taught, "All things in the universe, including lands and rivers, seas and skies express Buddha nature [that is, divine nature]. Everything is Buddha nature." Jesus emphasized this in terms of loving everyone equally, but did not include the different stages of love. Shakyamuni taught both ideas: that we are all equal and that there are different stages of enlightenment.

The Developmental Stages of Love and Enlightenment in Christianity and Buddhism

Instinctive Love

Just as there are stages of enlightenment in the Eightfold Path, there are also stages of love. The most basic stage is instinctive love: familiar love—the love for parents, siblings, a spouse, children, and other relatives; and sexual love. Instinctive love occupies 80 to 90 percent of people's attention.

Most people think that love is something you receive from others, but the desire to be loved is not true love, but merely a thirst. Buddhism sees this sort of love as attachment that often brings suffering. Jesus acknowledged the existence of instinctive love, but focused on the love that is a step higher—love of one's neighbor.

Instinctive love stems from the spirit world of the fourth dimension. If this love goes in the wrong direction, it becomes an attachment, which creates a hell in the fourth dimension. Those who have made mistakes in sexual love go to the Hell of Lust after death, and there they learn the lessons from the negative aspects of instinctive love. On the other hand, those who lived only in the state of instinctive love, but were able to gain peace of mind, go to the Astral Realm of the fourth dimension, which is a part of heaven. So instinctive love belongs to the fourth dimension, which is easy for everyone to reach after death. Since everyone can at least return to this dimension, going back to this realm should not be the final goal of our lives on earth. The world we are aiming for is the world of enlightenment, which is at a higher level.

Fundamental Love

The next level of love is fundamental love. It is higher than instinctive love, which often entails receiving from others or being loved by others, and belongs to the fifth dimension.

The fifth dimension is called the Realm of the Good, and its inhabitants understand that the essence of love is not receiving from those they love, but giving and being kind to others. This means loving not only your family, but also the people you meet in the course of your life—at your workplace or school, or elsewhere in society. People who understand this return to the fifth dimension.

You've probably thought about love on many occasions in your life. Is your understanding of love only a thirst for others' love or is it love that gives? Your answer indicates at what stage of love you are.

Spiritually Nurturing Love

Beyond fundamental love is spiritually nurturing love, which exists in the Light Realm of the sixth dimension. This is a love that guides people; it is a leader's or teacher's love, which brings out the divine, or Buddha nature, within people and enhances their spiritual development. In order to practice spiritually nurturing love and lead others, you must be independent and not need to rely on other people. A leader must refine his or her character and be exceptional. As Jesus said, "If a blind man leads a blind man, both will fall into a pit" (Matthew 15:14).

Spiritually nurturing love is the love of those who have studied and worked diligently to be able to guide others, such as entrepreneurs, teachers, artists, writers, doctors, judges, lawyers, and politicians.

Unfortunately, these kinds of people today seem concerned only with their own reputations and status. How many business owners are practicing spiritually nurturing love? A business executive should be a guiding light, someone able to lead employees. A leader should be of high caliber and have the ability to guide those who are following. The ability to make money is not enough.

Spiritually nurturing love is more difficult to practice. Leaders with true ability, who are guiding others and practicing love that gives, will return to the sixth dimension of heaven, the Realm of Light.

Forgiving Love

There are still higher worlds. The next world is the Bodhisattva Realm of the seventh dimension. Bodhisattvas are those who have attained a certain level of enlightenment on their own, passing beyond the sixth dimension. They have removed the rust from their minds, reached the state of Arhat, and radiate light. With undaunted spirit, they have taken the courageous first steps toward living a life of selflessness, a life dedicated to others. Not only are they superior to others in a worldly sense, but they have also reached the next spiritual stage.

When we live without any spiritual experiences, receiving only a worldly education and having only mundane thoughts and habits, it is difficult to live for others and manifest love as vast as an ocean. Only through a spiritual awakening or an encounter with a great teacher can we reach a religious state of mind and cultivate generosity. Those who have established such a true self can be truly kind to others who have not yet reached the same level. Only when you have reached this stage can you truly forgive others.

Love that gives may not seem difficult to practice. If those with a high social status—professors, doctors, and business executives, for example—work hard, it will not take them long to practice spiritually nurturing love. However, they may find it challenging, and have difficulty forgiving people who stand in their way, as Jesus taught. It is easy for managers to love and guide employees who accept their ideas, but they may resent employees who disagree with them, and may want to punish or demote them.

A good test of whether you can make the leap from spiritually nurturing love to forgiving love is the way you treat your opponents. As long as you view others as enemies, you cannot forgive them. As long as you regard someone as equally powerful or stronger than you, you cannot forgive that person. When you forgive someone who is at a higher spiritual level, this is merely to console yourself; it is not forgiving love. But when you have developed a heart that is big enough to embrace others, and have jumped to a higher spiritual level that embodies the light, you are able to view those who suffer in this world with kindness and compassion, as God does. This is the state of mind of the Bodhisattva.

In the stage of forgiving love, one person forgives another from a position of superiority. For example, a religious leader who encounters doubt or abuse from others might forgive them by thinking that they simply do not know the Truth. At that moment, the leader feels superior.

To achieve forgiving love, one must be more spiritually advanced than others, but this very requirement is also a limitation. A person may think, "People criticize me because they have not yet awakened to the Truth. Because I understand the Truth, I forgive them." This generous way of thinking embraces others, but maintains a sense of being superior, so there is still a stage further to go, which is even higher than the forgiving love that Jesus taught. It is the love of the Tathagata, the love that corresponds to the eighth dimension.

Love Incarnate

The love of Tathagata, or love incarnate, expresses the light of God; it is no longer a one-to-one love, but a love for everyone. A person who has attained the stage of Tathagata radiates boundless love in all directions, and that person's existence itself is love. This is the love embodied by the great figures whose names have lasted throughout history, such as the great Greek philosopher Socrates, who has influenced 2,400 years of history. In recent years, other great figures have brought light to the world: the great humanitarian Albert Schweitzer (1875–1965), and Thomas Edison (1847–1931), who contributed to the advancement of science and technology. The very existence of these great figures is an expression of love for all humanity.

The goal of your spiritual training on earth is to progress through the earlier stages of love—fundamental love, spiritually nurturing love, and forgiving love—to love incarnate, so that your very existence is a blessing to all humankind. With this love you are not living merely as a human being, but as a representative of God, a manifestation of light. Aim to embody this love, and to usher in a new epoch.

Even higher than these is the ninth dimension love of the savior, but this love is beyond the reach of people on earth.

Many religious leaders attempt to preach this level of love, but before teaching love of the savior, they themselves must progress through the stages of instinctive love, fundamental love, spiritually nurturing love, forgiving love, and love incarnate. Without having fulfilled each of these stages, it is impossible for them to embrace and promote the love of the savior.

Continue to study the Truth, using these four stages of love as guidelines for your spiritual development.

THREE

The Principle of
the Mind

The Teachings of the Mind

In the first chapter, I introduced the Fourfold Path, or the principles of happiness, which are love, wisdom, self-reflection, and progress. Chapter 2 was on the principle of love, the first principle of happiness.

This chapter should have been on the second principle, the principle of wisdom. However, I chose the principle of the mind as the next topic, because unless you understand your own inner world, your own mind, all knowledge is meaningless. The principle of wisdom is immensely vast, but if you become absorbed in the breadth of the Law, simply accumulating knowledge without understanding, you cannot make any spiritual progress.

Before discussing the principle of the mind, I would like to refer to my book *The Golden Laws*, which reveals the history of the angels of light and clarifies the historical background of my teachings.

It is not my intention to add yet one more religious sect to the already enormous number. As I make clear in *The Golden Laws*, our mission is to examine past civilizations and cultures that have flourished in many forms, and lead the way to the future of humanity in the twenty-first century and beyond.

Our motto at Happy Science is "From foundations to pillars, from the inside to the outside." I emphasize the importance of creating a firm foundation before building pillars, because a castle built on sand will soon collapse, no matter how grand its appearance. This applies to individuals as well as to organizations and teachings. Without a firm base, it is impossible to build anything of significance.

It is important to know the grand scale of the Law, but first we should look within. Unless we first establish an inner strength and understand our own minds, we will never be able to make progress through knowledge alone, no matter how much we learn about prehistory, human history, or the great figures of the past.

At Happy Science, we hold exploration of Right Mind to be fundamental, the most important philosophy in pursuing the four principles: love, wisdom, self-reflection, and progress. Understanding Right Mind is the first step to the enlightenment of individuals. The Truth is the same as it was in the time of Shakyamuni Buddha. The enlightenment of individuals comes first, then the enlightenment of the whole follows. Only after people refine their minds and overcome their limitations are they able to direct their vision outward: from themselves to others, from others to the visible world, and from the visible to the unseen world.

In the third chapter of *The Golden Laws,* "Eternal Mountains and Rivers," I briefly explain Shakyamuni's Buddhist teachings, which focus on the idea that benefiting the self benefits others. There is no such thing as universal happiness, independent of the happiness of each individual. So each of us should first look within and take responsibility for our own happiness or unhappiness, the result of our thoughts and actions. Without that responsibility and knowledge, how can we bring happiness to others? We should not be too concerned with other people's problems before we have sorted out our own.

Your first aim must be to master the teachings on refining your mind and soul. Seventy to 80 percent of your spiritual discipline should be dedicated to this goal. Without this effort, no matter how much historical knowledge you acquire, you will never be able to attain enlightenment.

Only by looking within, attaining your own enlightenment and broadening your own perspective, will you be able to develop greatness and nobility of character. Always remember these steps in order to progress.

The True Nature of the Mind and Its Structure

The prerequisite for becoming a member of our movement is the willingness to explore Right Mind every day. What does "right" mean in this context? Does it simply mean "not wrong," or does it have a deeper meaning? In Happy Science it means the rightness that human beings originally possessed. Our aim in exploring Right Mind is to restore the mind to its original, God-given state.

Although the exact time of creation of each soul varies, human souls were created several billion years ago when, in a corner of the galaxy, the great light of God was scattered in small photons. This was the beginning of the creation of humankind. Each of these particles of light was endowed with individuality, dispersed, and, over the course of time, began to develop its own consciousness and experience its own unique life. We need to remember our origins and the nature that we were endowed with at the time of our creation.

In my publications on the Truth, I describe the various realms that exist in heaven. Our ultimate goal is not simply to create a similar world on earth, but to realize a world more perfect than heaven, a world that existed at the beginning of time, when we enjoyed complete freedom of the soul. Now is a turning point in our quest to restore this freedom and the true nature of the soul that was once ours.

What is the essential nature of the soul? What was our original state? How can we restore this original state?

The soul originates from God and essentially possesses the same qualities as God. God is essentially light itself. This light is not like the light of a lamp; it has attributes such as love, compassion, wisdom, and prosperity, which shine like the facets of a diamond. Most spiritual leaders cannot explain all of these brilliant facets, but choose to focus on only one of them. However, understanding the true nature of the whole diamond is the true objective of spiritual discipline.

This is not a quest for something that exists outside of you. You may think that the other world, the fourth dimension upward, is an invisible world that exists somewhere high in the sky. Perhaps you imagine that after you shed your physical body, you will return to the world of the soul that exists far beyond this world. But the truth is that all the realms of the other world exist within your mind.

Although this is just an external appearance and does not represent the ultimately true nature of mind, if your spiritual eyes are open, your mind looks like a balloon that is constantly changing shape. If your mind is harmonized, it appears beautifully round, like a full moon or a ball.

On the other hand, if your mind is out of balance, the ball appears more or less distorted. In some people, the area of emotion has grown disproportionately large, while others have an overwhelmingly large intellectual area. For example, if a person has studied the Truth only in an academic way, the area in the mind that governs intellect has become swollen.

There is also an area that governs reason. In the minds of people who always see things dispassionately, this area is disproportionately large, and these people rarely experience profound emotions.

At the top of the ball-shaped mind is the area that governs thought. It is here that we create a wide variety of thoughts, and this is the part that causes most individual human suffering.

Medical science accepts that the mind exists in the cerebral cortex of the brain, but this isn't true. You don't think with your brain. The brain is simply an information control center, a computer room for processing data. When it is damaged and cannot function properly, a person loses control of actions, speech, and judgment. The damage to the computer has nothing to do with the user, but only affects the separate entity that operates the computer and inputs data. Many people would agree that both sadness and joy well up from the chest, not from the head. So it seems reasonable to say the mind is located somewhere near the heart, rather than in the head.

Mind, Soul, and Spirit

The words *soul, spirit,* and *mind* are often used interchangeably. People have only a superficial understanding of these words, and no concrete idea of their true nature. Sometimes they all represent the same thing, and at other times, they refer to different things. For example, when a newspaper survey asked the question "Do you believe in spiritual beings?" about 20 percent of respondents answered that they did and about 50 percent answered that spiritual beings probably existed, but that they weren't sure. On the other hand, when asked "Do you think that the mind exists?" 99 percent answered yes, and most also agreed that human beings possess a mental function.

The mind is the central part of the human soul, the core of the spiritual body. The soul and the mind cannot be seen as physical forms; they are spiritual entities. To spiritual sight, the mind looks like a ball about one foot in diameter, and it is located at the center of the soul, which is shaped exactly like the physical body.

What, then, is the difference between the soul and the spirit? The soul has a distinctive human shape and its own individuality, while the spirit is freer in form.

Human spirits and animal spirits differ somewhat. The spirits of animals are not as individualized as those of humans. How individual they become depends on the level of each animal's consciousness. When a dog, for example, loses its life on earth and goes to the other world, if it was very conscious of its individuality throughout its incarnations, it will continue to live as a separate canine spirit. If it is unconscious of its individuality, however, it will become part of a group of dozens of canine spirits. In heaven, animal spirits of a similar consciousness form one collective consciousness, without any individuality, and when it is time to reincarnate, one part of the group separates to be born on earth.

Plants also have spirits. To those who have spiritual sight, the spirits of plants look like small human beings, similar to sprites that can see and talk. But not many plants are individualized, so when they leave this earth and return to heaven, they usually live together in groups. On the other hand, big ancient trees that have lived for hundreds of years, watching centuries of human history, develop a consciousness similar to that of humans, so when they return to heaven, each continues to live as an individual tree consciousness.

The Evolution of Spiritual Awareness

The Fourth Dimension (the Posthumous Realm)

In the case of human beings, things are more complicated. A human soul is a life-size entity dwelling in a physical body. After leaving this world, most souls continue to retain that physical body. Some, however, gradually begin to realize that the soul does not need that body to exist. The inhabitants of the Posthumous Realm of the fourth dimension lead lives similar to those of people on earth, even after they have returned to the other world. They still see themselves with a physical body, which limits their level of consciousness. They feel uncomfortable if they do not have arms and legs, or do not stand on the ground. Some even eat three meals a day and feel sleepy at night.

The Fifth Dimension (the Realm of the Good)

As you go to higher realms—the fifth, sixth, seventh, and eighth dimensions—the situation changes. The fifth dimension, or the Realm of the Good, is a world where good-natured, harmonious people return. Even in this realm, the inhabitants continue their spiritual discipline in human form for about 90 percent of the time. But through occasional mysterious experiences, they begin to realize that they are not the same as they believed themselves to be; they have no need to walk on the earth, and even if they jump off a cliff will not die. They begin to realize they have the ability to move freely to any place they wish.

In the fourth dimension, souls under the guidance of various spirits occasionally appear wherever they want or meet whomever they wish, but these experiences are only by chance. In the fifth dimension, souls are able to do this more or less at will. They begin to realize through their own experiences that they can exist without a human form, and become aware that they are actually spiritual beings. They are still concerned about their physical bodies, however, and do not feel comfortable if, for example, they are not the same height as they were while on earth.

The Sixth Dimension (the Light Realm)

Above this is the Light Realm of the sixth dimension. There are different levels of consciousness in this realm, but to live here you must believe that the world you live in is God's creation and it is governed by the Truth that originates from him. In the sixth dimension, many strive to refine their souls through the study of the Truth. As they continue their studies, they gradually free themselves from the physical senses they had while on earth. On the basis of their knowledge of the Truth, they begin to test what they have learned.

Those who have reached this stage become aware that their power is not as limited as the power of people on earth. They study the will from different angles, and angels of light who take on the role of teachers instruct them about the nature and the power of will.

They first learn by experience. The inhabitants of the sixth dimension have learned that they can create anything with their own will, and actually put this into practice. They materialize an image by holding it in their mind, for example, making a drinking glass appear on a desk.

The inhabitants of the fourth and fifth dimensions have similar experiences, but they do not fully recognize that they are able to create things. Spirits in the sixth dimension, on the other hand, are fully aware of their creative ability.

Once it becomes easy to manifest that glass, they may try to create a patterned drinking glass. When they have succeeded in that, they wonder if they can produce water in the glass, and water appears. When the glass is filled with water, they drink it and find that it tastes the same as the water they used to drink on earth. In this way they become confident that they can produce a glass of water through the power of their own will.

For decades or hundreds of years, they continue this kind of practice. After a while, they become bored with producing glasses of water and begin to think of making other things. Spirits who are interested in clothes may wonder if they can create clothing that has a particular pattern. They imagine, for example, a shirt with polka dots and try to create it. At first they may misfire and create a shirt with stripes. So then they decide to practice by producing a plain white shirt. Once they actually master this, they try creating trousers of their favorite design. Upon succeeding, they go back to polka dots, this time with the intention of making twenty dots. Perhaps only seventeen come out and they wonder what happened to the other three.

As they continue to practice, they learn that they can create personal belongings by means of will power. They then think they might be able to produce things other than clothes: a watch, for example. They start making an elaborate watch. Those who are more advanced in their training can create an excellent watch immediately, whereas beginners have difficulty.

At this stage, spirits start thinking: "Until now I haven't felt comfortable unless my form in the mirror is the same as it was on earth. But maybe I could change my appearance and take another form." A spirit who was comfortable being an average height begins to wonder if it could grow to the height of seven feet. Its body grows taller and taller until it has reached that height, and it walks around at that size. The first experience usually ends with the spirit, uncomfortable with this new form, returning to its more comfortable, original form. But as time goes by, it gets accustomed to this kind of experience and begins to will itself to grow taller. It may even try to lengthen its arms, and watch its arms grow as expected. Through these experiences, spirits in the sixth dimension come to realize that the physical body is not their true, ultimate nature.

The spirits of the sixth dimension are categorized as "high spirits." In the course of their studies they are taught that they should not only concentrate on their own studies, but also guide people on earth. The sixth dimension is a wonderful place, but spirits are encouraged to move on. The spirits from higher dimensions tell them, "You should aim to proceed to the Bodhisattva Realm of the seventh dimension to learn to help others." The spirits of the sixth dimension begin to think, "Now that I am accustomed to life here, I would like to learn to help people," and they are assigned roles as the guardians and guiding spirits of people on earth.

A guardian spirit is a part of one's own soul, and a guiding spirit is a spirit that has a specialized ability in a particular field and guides those on earth when necessary. If a person on earth who is originally from the fourth or fifth dimension receives guidance from a guiding spirit of the sixth dimension, he or she will be able to see and judge things from a higher perspective.

Through inspiration, the spirits of the sixth dimension may provide a scholar with the idea for the theme of his or her thesis, a poet with fresh ideas or apt words, and an artist with unique images for paintings. Wonderful works of art owe a great deal to this kind of inspiration, and it is mostly spirits in the sixth dimension who are in charge of vocational and professional guidance. After they have gone through a certain level of spiritual development in the other world, they begin to guide people on earth.

Some people on earth have the ability to see spiritual phenomena and witness the forms of guiding spirits. As guiding spirits know that their true nature is not physical, when guiding people on earth they choose to take a godlike form rather than appearing dressed in business suits. For example, when appearing before religious leaders, they take the form of angelic beings.

As I indicated in *The Laws of the Sun,* on the reverse side of the major realm of the sixth dimension is the realm known as Minor Heaven, the realm inhabited by Tengu (long-nosed spirits living in mountains that possess spiritual powers) and Sennin (hermit wizards).

In some areas in these realms, the inhabitants concentrate on enhancing their psychic powers and transforming themselves at will. As they become able to change themselves into something other than human beings, they gradually become aware of their true nature and begin to understand that they are spiritual beings.

The Seventh Dimension (the Bodhisattva Realm)

After going through the fifth and sixth dimensions, and having reached the Bodhisattva Realm of the seventh dimension, spirits have further experiences that convince them that their true nature is not corporeal. Bodhisattvas dedicate themselves to loving acts and to saving many people, so they are very busy fulfilling various duties. They gradually come to feel that having a human form is quite inconvenient. As long as they are pursuing their own studies, they have no problem taking a human form; otherwise they prefer working in an easier form. At times they shed their human form and embody the will.

Some Bodhisattvas belong to the group of medical spirits, and take charge of healing illnesses. When they are busy healing people, they sometimes become pure energy of will, a consciousness wanting to help those who work in the medical field. As they labor from morning till night, they forget that they are human spirits and become totally absorbed in performing acts of love. When they suddenly become aware of themselves, meaning that they remember the fact that they are human spirits and used to take a human form, those who are Bodhisattvas begin to have these sorts of experiences intermittently. This is how they recognize themselves to be spiritual beings.

The Eighth Dimension (the Tathagata Realm)

When Bodhisattvas reach the Tathagata Realm of the eighth dimension, they attain an even higher level of consciousness. You understand the soul and spirit through physical perception alone, but Tathagatas understand that a human is not a physical being.

In the seventh dimension, Bodhisattvas still have a human shape and lead individual lives, but things are different for the spirits of Tathagatas. They recognize themselves as the embodiment of the Law, and rather than existing as individuals, they are the Tathagata consciousness itself.

What is Tathagata consciousness? There are seven colors in the spectrum of divine light. Among them are the white light of love and the red light of Moses—leadership. The Chinese philosophers Lao-tzu and Chuang-tzu belong to the green light of harmony, while Confucius and Japanese Shinto gods belong to the violet light of reverence. The spirits of the Tathagata Realm work as pure consciousness, representing these lights. However, when they communicate with people on earth or when they appear before people as spirits, they take on a human form. In the Tathagata Realm they still enjoy individual private life, reading books or taking walks, but for the most part they work as pure consciousness.

The eighth-dimensional Tathagatas are highly spiritually advanced, and although they exist as a larger consciousness rather than individual souls, occasionally a Tathagata will recall former memories and take on a human form.

As I mentioned in *The Laws of the Sun,* the enlightenment of Tathagatas is expressed as "one is many, many are one." This means that a Tathagata spirit can just as easily be five or ten entities, and five or ten entities can function as one. Tathagatas recognize themselves to be as many entities as are needed for a particular function.

In the world of Tathagata, spirits do not have one-on-one relationships as human beings do, but are able to split into as many entities as necessary. Before attaining the Tathagata level, they advanced through many spiritual levels, had experiences in the fourth and fifth dimensions, and perhaps even experienced hell. Through all these experiences, they learned the true nature of the spirit and reached a level of awareness that enables them to fulfill their role as pure consciousness.

The Ninth Dimension (the Cosmic Realm)

Above this is the ninth dimension, where each consciousness is even more vast. In the Tathagata Realm of the eighth dimension, spirits can manifest as a multitude of personalities for a particular purpose, but in the ninth dimension, one consciousness is able to take on many personalities for a multitude of purposes. The consciousness of the ninth dimension creates many dams within one great pool, each dam with a name: for example, Shakyamuni Buddha, Jesus Christ, or Moses. Each of these dams has particular characteristics and stores a great amount of water to be released into rivers of light when necessary. The water flows to the places where it is needed. The dam is a source of the Law.

It may be hard to form a clear image of the spirits of the ninth dimension. They do not consist of one core spirit and five branch spirits, but rather, if they wish, can separate themselves into millions of entities. Their human awareness has almost faded away, but since they have also experienced living as human beings, they are able to manifest a consciousness with a personality, if necessary. Their true nature, however, is like a dam of a great river, and the composition of the water stored differs from dam to dam.

Thus, each of us on earth can be compared to a particle of water that has flowed from a huge dam down to the mouth of a river. If a grand Tathagata can be symbolized by a dam, perhaps you can imagine how far beyond the human sphere the God of Creation is.

The Exploration of Right Mind

Balancing the Mind

A soul with a human shape progresses to become a spirit without a human form, then a consciousness with a purpose, and eventually the source of the Law. In this way, as we trace it back to its origin, we come to understand the nature of the mind.

Now, turning away from the multidimensional world back to this world, what should we do, as beings living on earth? We know that there are ultimately great consciousnesses like dams, acting out their roles. However, at present we are not consciousnesses soaring in the sky; we are confined to limited physical bodies. How can we understand our true nature and make the most of it in our everyday lives? The soul is essentially life energy that can expand to become as infinite as the universe, and it can also contract to become as tiny as a mustard seed. We are unable, however, to understand our consciousness if it is the size of a seed—it is too small to contemplate. We need to focus on the consciousness, or soul, dwelling in the physical body, and control it. To rule the soul that dwells in the physical body, we must first try to govern the mind, for the mind is the core of the soul.

What are the areas that exist in the mind? There are different areas for emotions or sensibility, will, intellect, and reason. When you look into your inner self, you should first check the balance of your mind, and whether these areas are well balanced. Is the emotional area of your mind swollen? Are you emotionally stable throughout the day? Do you have difficulty controlling your emotions?

What about the area of will? Will is determination to realize your intentions. Although it is good to have a strong will, check to see that you don't always insist on getting your own way, or cannot understand the feelings of others. Having a cast-iron will is not necessarily bad, but are you flexible enough to make changes when necessary?

There is also the area of intellect. True intellect includes the spiritual wisdom that is emphasized in Buddhism. However, rather than becoming teachers of the soul, some Buddhist priests become merely interpreters of sutras, and some Christian priests and ministers focus only on the study of the Bible and church doctrine. You should make sure that the intellectual area of your mind has not become distorted or bloated.

Finally, check the area of reason. Reason plays the role of a compass, steering the course of a life in the right direction. But if the area of reason becomes overdeveloped, you tend to be aloof and critical, coolly analyzing others and their actions and criticizing their faults. Because you forget that all human souls are essentially brothers and sisters, and that as children of God we are one with each other, you start to look at people and events using reason alone.

Make sure that the areas of will, emotion, intellect, and reason are well balanced, and that together they form a perfectly round ball, for this is the first step in exploring Right Mind.

Purify Your Thought Tape

The next step is to remove any clouds of thought hanging over the mind. Surrounding the mind is what is called a "thought tape," and the condition of this tape determines whether or not you are happy in the course of your life.

You have probably learned what constitutes good thoughts and bad thoughts. For instance, tenderness, kindness, sympathy, and love for others are good; complaint, anger, jealousy, and envy are bad. These negative thoughts, as well as selfish thoughts and a desire for self-preservation, will create clouds over the thought tape of the mind. The clouds of these wrong thoughts block God's light.

The true nature of God's will is the light of the Great Tathagata (Amitabha) that illuminates everything in all ways, without discrimination. This light is unobstructed life energy that pours out in all directions, but is still able to be blocked.

As described in *The Golden Laws,* God's light demonstrates both affinity and exclusivity. God's light has an affinity to anything that corresponds to the qualities dwelling in the light, and it excludes anything negative that does not correspond to these qualities. This is the divine Law that results in the problems that arise with the thought tape of the mind.

The light that comes from heaven is God's light, or energy, while the energy with which you create a roof is the creative energy that is given to all of God's children. Both energies originate from the same source. Because you have, in essence, the same freedom to create as God, in whom you have your origin, you can create a roof that blocks the sunlight by means of your own thoughts.

In the course of our lives, we unconsciously accumulate negative thoughts, creating mental clouds that block light and cause our minds to become distorted. No matter how hard your guardian or guiding spirits try to help you correct the course of your life, the clouds over your mind will occlude even their guiding light. As a result of your own choices, you create clouds in your mind, block out the light, and live in darkness.

To become happy, you need to remove these clouds of thought through your own efforts, since you alone created them. If your house becomes messy, whose responsibility is it to clean it? Would you telephone Town Hall to send a cleaning crew? No, you are the one who must clean your own house.

I have received letters from members of a certain religious group claiming that God saves everyone, and that pain and suffering occur merely to cancel out bad karma. Pain and suffering actually arise because people create the causes themselves. They produce the clouds of thought that hinder God's light, and become unable to receive the guidance of their guardian and guiding spirits. As a result, they are likely to live their lives wrongly and end up in hell.

The causes of pain and suffering do not lie with others or the outside world; you yourself create them. Since you have created your own suffering, you must remove it yourself. However, prayer alone will never clear the clouds from your thoughts.

Do not interpret God's love to mean that you can do whatever you want because any pain or suffering is bound to disappear. Deep in your soul, you need to understand that your suffering is the result of clouds over your thoughts, and unless these clouds are cleared away, you can never live in the right way, as a child of God. The errors you have made through your own decisions must be corrected while you are alive in this world. Through your own effort, reflect on your thoughts and deeds and correct them; only you can save yourself. This practice is absolutely essential. Remember the two most important points in the principle of the mind: first, keep the different areas of the mind in balance; next, find the clouds of thought, remove them through your own efforts using self-reflection, and restore your mind to its original state. There is no other path to true happiness.

◀ PART TWO ▶

True Awakening

Realizing enlightenment is not easy. However, enlightenment achieved after overcoming challenges is true happiness. Humans truly are spiritual beings. When you return to the spirit world, the only thing you can take with you is your mind. For this reason, enlightenment must be the purpose of life, because it is an inner state of complete happiness. Do not think of your present state as happiness if you have not developed spiritually or experienced a true awakening, for without these experiences, happiness is only an illusion.

The principles of enlightenment, progress, and wisdom are the essence of the Laws. These principles are the compass of the mind, essential to those who dedicate themselves to spiritual refinement based on Truth. Souls must be firm and steady; this creates harmony and keeps them from falling as they advance. In particular, the idea of progress through the Middle Way and the outline of the developmental stages of wisdom will surely guarantee the eternal evolution of your soul.

FOUR

The Principle of Enlightenment

Aspiring to Seek the Truth

Happy Science was established on October 6, 1986, and within a year
the movement had grown more rapidly than I had expected. Initially,
I had planned to limit the number of members, but more and more
people applied. Despite my wish that the organization operate quietly
for the first few years, every month thousands of letters poured in.
When I thought about the long-term future of the movement, I realized that unless we established firm foundations based on a very clear
vision, our movement would be consumed by its own enormous energy.
So I resolved to manage it rigorously. Happy Science is a very demanding organization, and we maintain high standards. At the beginning, to
become a member of our organization, an applicant had to read at least
ten of my books and write an essay explaining why he or she wanted
to join. Most applicants, however, read more than twenty books. I was
impressed by the great enthusiasm of those who went above and beyond,
despite our intention to control the growth of membership.

Once people were admitted as members, they continued to strive to
progress spiritually. In the first year, we organized a retreat seminar in
May, and held a Level 1 seminar test in August and a Level 2 seminar

test in September. The members had enormous enthusiasm for learning the Truth. Each time I read essays they had written on the Truth, I found the quality had improved. In the initial stages, when membership was less than two or three thousand, I introduced an examination system to create a framework for our activities, from which I would plan the future development of the organization. Until the framework was in place, I would have to control the expansion of the organization.

When membership increased to tens of thousands, I knew I would no longer be able to give individual instruction, so I wanted those who had gathered in the early stages to develop themselves as leaders, and to guide newcomers. Happy Science was unique in that it had an examination system for lay members; other groups may have exams for clergy, but they have none for members. Level 1, 2, and 3 seminars, which cover basic to advanced levels, all include a lecture and an essay to be graded after the seminar. The purposes of these seminars are to provide members with opportunities to acquire more knowledge of the Truth and to refine their souls.

Establishing a New System of Values

While some of our members understand why we hold these kinds of examinations, others may not. Those who take the tests score fairly consistently, but the people who usually do best are not necessarily the most intellectual. The results reflect the members' strong yearning to find the Truth and their enthusiasm for the pursuit of enlightenment. They also show that in a random sampling of people, some possess a certain level of understanding of the Truth that has nothing to do with intelligence, education, status, or income.

Because Happy Science has strict management policies, we seem to have gained the trust of much of society. Many of our members are professors, doctors, other professionals, and intellectuals.

Doctors who have graduated from medical school are usually intelligent, and would be expected to score well on our seminar tests, but they don't necessarily achieve the highest scores. This is difficult for highly educated people to understand; they think, "I'm an intelligent person. Why can't I get a high score?" This issue arises from our attempt to establish a new system of values, one that contradicts the values most people take for granted.

Earthly values do not always reflect the values of the heavenly world. If you think of the worldly value system as a pyramid, in many areas it is upside down, shaped like an inverted triangle. People who are doing absolutely nothing of worth in God's eyes are, in some cases, the most highly respected. Most people on earth don't understand what is or isn't of true value. For instance, some people think it important to become famous or appear on TV, while others place a high value on working for a major company with a good reputation.

When you return to the other world, your position there will have absolutely nothing to do with your social status in this world. Sometimes it can be quite the reverse. Jesus said, "I tell you the truth, unless you change and become like little children, you will never enter the kingdom of heaven" (Matthew 18:3). When some see young people getting top scores, they protest, insisting, "I have been seeking enlightenment through many different religions for more than ten years, so my level of enlightenment should be higher than a young person's." Entering the gates of heaven is not dependent on age. A person who has accumulated many experiences will not necessarily go to a higher realm in heaven than someone who is young and inexperienced. A person who has been a company president and had a lot of influence does not necessarily go to a higher realm.

The true values of the Real World are completely different from the values of this world, so you cannot judge a person's level by social status or academic background alone. Many leaders throughout history have attempted to reveal the standards and values of the Real World, but no one has been successful in revealing the whole picture. My true mission in the heavenly world is to establish and uphold the standard of values based on the divine Law. Here on earth, one of my main tasks is to demonstrate true values as seen through the eyes of God, to shine light on values that until now have been in darkness. Although you may think that the world of Truth is wonderful, perhaps you are uncomfortable speaking about it openly in your workplace, or among family and friends. You may feel it would not be to your advantage to reveal your interest in spirituality, or worry it might negatively influence your career or relationships.

When we are doing what is of greatest value, why should we be worried if others know about it? Society's "norms" must be wrong. If the current norms are mistaken, we need to change them. We at Happy Science are presenting a new standard of values, and demonstrating how fragile the current societal norms are. Now is the time to show the world what true values are, and what kind of people are truly worthy of respect. On passing over to the other world, those who hold themselves in high regard in this world will realize how unimportant they truly are. No matter how important they may have been or how high the positions they held in this world, they will come to realize they are but tiny beings before the great guiding spirits of light.* In the presence of angels of light they feel so small that a mere glimpse of the light of these angels prompts them to look closely at their own being.† This experience is beyond description. Because they did not know the Truth, they become less in the other world. But since they alone are responsible for their ignorance, they cannot make any excuses for not knowing the Truth, no matter how small they become when they return to the other world. While they were living on earth, opportunities to encounter the Truth and clues to achieve enlightenment were all around them. They mocked those chances and scoffed at those opportunities, deriding the clues as complete nonsense.

Once in the other world, reflecting on their lives on earth will help people to fully understand how ignorant they were.

---

*The great guiding spirits of light are those who reside in the Tathagata Realm of the eighth dimensional world and higher. They have the ability to create a culture or civilization with their teachings.
†In the spirit world, the higher the spiritual level, the more light a spirit emits.

Coming into Contact with the Truth

Enlightenment starts with knowing. You must know God, the will of God, and the teachings that flow from God's mind. Without this understanding, you will never be able to grasp any of the clues to enlightenment. There are many methods for attaining enlightenment, but you will never be able to reach this state simply by undertaking a thousand-day walk in the mountains or sitting beneath a waterfall, as many Buddhist seekers do. The path that leads to enlightenment is the path that leads to spiritual awareness,* and to attain spiritual awareness you have to know about something that is beyond this world. When you have experienced the total reversal of your worldly values and encountered the Truth, you can be said to have taken the first step toward enlightenment.

"Knowing" means first getting in touch with the world of Truth. There are no excuses for ignorance of the Truth. One opportunity to encounter it lies in reading my books of Truth or listening to my lectures; these books and lectures are arrows of light shot from the world of Truth. In order to correct the value system of this world, we must give people as many opportunities as possible to read books of Truth. Whether or not readers of these books will awaken to the Truth is up to them, but the task of angels of light is, at the very least, to provide opportunities for enlightenment. The Law is rarely taught, so when it is taught, a firm foundation must be laid so that the Law will lead people to enlightenment, not only in this age, but also for thousands of years to come. You are not the only readers I have in mind. A part of my task is to also enlighten those who will live in the future.

No matter how this world will change in the future, the Laws of the mind are universal. The Truth is eternal and unchanging, and our mission is to awaken people to it. The teachings will become a guiding light for people in times to come, so I will never compromise with the

---

*Spiritual awareness is the awakening to the true self, with the knowledge that humans are spiritual beings and children of God.

norms of modern society. Even if the times or the environment change, no matter what kind of world unfolds, our mission is to point to what is unchanging in the midst of change.

Transmission of the Law

If this is our mission, we must have a broad perspective; we need to consider what we should leave behind for the age to come, the Golden Age of the future. (See chapter 5 of *The Laws of the Sun*.) This is not only my task, but yours as well. The Law is the pillar, the basis of all values, but it is not something fixed or unmoving; rather, it rotates and radiates light of different colors. To receive this light, we need to be able to accept the light of each of these colors unfolding like a rainbow,[1] and pass them on to others. This requires an active effort. This means that those of you who are reading this message should not be content just to read it. Once you have read it, you must then change your own mind. You have not truly understood my words until your mind has been transformed. If you are touched deeply and something resonates in your heart, you have heard my words before, maybe in past lives on earth or in the other world. I am addressing the heart of each one of you; I am appealing to your soul.

I will leave this world in March 2037, just before the cherry blossoms reach full bloom. I will not incarnate again to teach the Law for another twenty-eight hundred years. My challenge is to live this life to the fullest in the years that are left to me. My mission is to spread the Truth as far as possible and to as many people as possible.

But it is not enough simply to spread the Truth far and wide.

The real challenge is to touch people's souls deeply and leave the Truth behind in solid form. To achieve this, I can't just shout out my message like a street preacher; the Law cannot be passed on simply by shaking hands with a lot of people.

How did Buddhism get passed down to us? It was the combined efforts of serious seekers who disciplined themselves and sought enlightenment. In an office, one person can do the work of five or six people at most. But in handing down the Law, the achievement and influence of just one person's life can be far greater. In the world of Truth, one person can be as powerful as ten thousand, or even one million. After my earthly life is over, the torch of Dharma will be handed on by seekers who have a mission, even if there is only one such person every ten or twenty years. This has been the basis of the transmission of Buddhism.

There are an enormous number of religious sects thriving all over the world. However, after the founders die, most of these groups lose their direction and collapse. The successors try to pass on the teachings as if they were an inheritance, like possessions, and attempt to maintain the structure, the property, and the lifestyle. This is a mistake—the Truth must be passed from one enlightened person to another. In history, Buddhism was transmitted from India to China and from China to Japan; blood relationships and institutional status had no place in the transmission of Buddha's teachings. The principle has always been "from one enlightened person to another."

The Japanese Buddhist priest Kukai (774–835 CE) went to China and studied esoteric teachings under the priest Master Hui-kuo (746–805) (see chapters 3 and 4 of *The Golden Laws*). Just before Master Hui-kuo passed away, he named Kukai as his successor. In the eyes of Hui-kuo's disciples, Kukai was an unknown stranger who had come across the sea to China. Hui-kuo was truly international and open-minded in the transmission of Buddha's teachings. When Master Hui-kuo handed on the torch of Dharma to Kukai before he passed away, his closest disciples were no doubt disappointed and envious. Those disciples had followed Master Hui-kuo for a long time, but the teacher did not select any of them to inherit the torch of Dharma; instead he chose a foreigner who had come to China only half a year before. The disciples had difficulty accepting that harsh truth.

However, inheriting the torch of Dharma demands complete belief. The path of enlightenment is like a narrow path across mountain peaks; the level of enlightenment cannot be allowed to drop below the peaks. It continues from mountaintop to mountaintop, from ridge to ridge. This path is unyielding. The transmission of the Law must not be influenced by personal considerations; whether or not the Law is passed on correctly is the key to determining the happiness or unhappiness of future generations, as well as the happiness of those who are living now. It allows no compromise.

Seekers of the Truth must realize that every day is a test; every day you walk this narrow path. Without complete belief, how can you save not only those who are living today, but also future generations? Even if the membership of our organization were to grow to millions, if the members were not serious in their search for enlightenment, this increase would have no meaning. One person who has attained a high level of enlightenment is of far greater benefit to humanity than many who merely dabble in enlightenment. This is a core idea in the transmission and succession of the Law.

There are absolutely no limits to learning the Truth. Seek the Truth with all your intellect, with all your passion, and with all your energy. Even if you already seek the Truth continuously, you must never be satisfied and never stop learning. There is something more you have not yet achieved. Many people will read this message, but each of you will understand it differently. If you convey the Truth with mistakes in interpretation, what effect will this have? You must first understand the rigor of the Law and of enlightenment.

Therefore, it is essential that we establish foundations before we start missionary work. I do not preach for entertainment; I preach so that each reader will acquire the knowledge to become an angel of light. So go back to the starting point and reflect on your resolve. Are you passionate and enthusiastic about our movement and its effect on others? Or are you a part of this movement only for what it may bring to you?

You must be willing to die for your cause. I'm not talking about the life and death of the body, but a spiritual death. Crucify your weakness that chooses the easy way. Crucify your mind that is swayed by worldly desires and easily deluded by immediate worldly gain. This is the true meaning of the biblical phrase "No one can see the kingdom of God unless he is born again" (John 3:3). Unless you have a strong, unswerving determination, you cannot really assimilate the Truth as your own. Until you awaken, you will never be able to awaken others.

How to Develop the Right Attitude for Successful Spiritual Practice

Love Is Invincible

We receive many telephone calls and letters from various religious groups. Some deliver threats, claiming that since our movement started their business has declined. These threats leave us unmoved; our commitment to our cause is stronger than that. Their motivation is to protect their earthly profits, whereas ours is to realize God's will on earth. In time, they will come to understand this difference in attitude.

We cannot distort the Truth for shallow reasons. The Truth is the Truth and what is right is right. God's will is God's will. The late Japanese Christian leader Kanzo Uchimura (1861–1930)[*2] declared that he would fight all enemies of the Truth. I feel the same way, but in my view, no one is the enemy of the Truth—there are only those who have awakened to the Truth and those who have yet to awaken.

On this earth there are no demons, nor is there any evil of real substance. Even those who seem to oppose us are not truly evil beings; they are not Satan, or demons, but simply those who have not yet awakened to the Truth. They, too, are children of God. There is no distinction between "good" and "bad" people, only between those whose eyes have been opened and those whose eyes are still closed. Human beings are not created so imperfect as to be evil by nature.

Kanzo Uchimura's determination to fight against all enemies of the Truth should be our model, yet if there is no enemy, then everyone is

---

*Kanzo Uchimura devoted himself to the spread of Christianity in Japan with the concept of "non-church Christianity."

on our side. Some are active supporters and others have not yet realized that they should be supporting our movement. Rather than fight against an enemy, we should remind people of the true Law that is deep within them and rekindle the torch in their hearts. We are determined to advance on our path; we will not fight, but nor will we compromise. We will hold a clear vision of the way in which the Truth will unfold on earth. This attitude and an indomitable spirit are essential. We must believe that love has no enemies. No matter how rigid a person's shell of self-protection, it can never be hard enough to shield someone against the spear of love. So when we act, we strive to find each person's divine nature.* Within each individual is the brilliance of the diamond that shines, the same brilliance that you have already discovered in yourself through endeavoring to refine your soul.

Loving others means loving the sacred radiance that shines within them—their true nature—which is the nature of a child of God. The divine nature that you find in others is the same nature that you discover in yourself. This is the true meaning of the saying "Self and others are one." The child of God discovers the child of God and the child of God loves the child of God. It is important to have a perspective that does not separate you from others.

The first step to attaining enlightenment is to discover the divine nature within you. Only those who have discovered their own divine inner nature can see the same divine nature in others. Those who have not yet discovered their divine inner nature cannot find it in others, much less help them to discover it.

The Theravada movement should not be separate from the Mahayana movement.† We must understand that the seed of the Mahayana movement already exists in Theravada. In *The Golden Laws,* I explained the essence of Shakyamuni's Buddhism in the teaching, "Benefiting the

---

*Everyone is a child of God; within each mind is the light of God.
†The Theravada and Mahayana movements are metaphorical expressions of the teachings that will lead people to enlightenment. Theravada represents teachings to increase individual enlightenment, whereas Mahayana represents teachings for saving others.

self benefits others."[3] In other words, first you should refine yourself, because that process benefits others. You must not protect your own ego or your own interests, but must find the divine nature within and make it shine. Then you will find the divine nature in others shining forth in response to the light within you. This teaching aims to reunite the self with others.

The Exploration of Right Mind

Now we need to consider how to discover our own inner light, the divine nature within each one of us. Since I created Happy Science, I have been advocating the exploration of Right Mind and the principles of happiness. The exploration of Right Mind is both the entrance to and the destination of the path of the Truth. This exploration is the pillar of your spiritual discipline on earth as well as the lifeline that connects you to God so that you will not drown in the worldly ocean of delusion.

Right Mind doesn't refer to rightness in the sense of right and wrong. Right is a value that appears through the process of uncovering the Truth. The deeper and harder you search for the Truth, the brighter rightness shines, and this "rightness" cannot be measured against a set of commandments that tells you "You may do this, but not that."

Throughout history, many guiding spirits of light who have descended to earth in the flesh have left commandments such as "You shall not kill," "You shall not steal," and "You shall not bear false witness." Moses and Shakyamuni gave commandments and indicated rules that seekers must observe; however, those commandments were not intended to differentiate right from wrong, but to serve as guideposts on the path to enlightenment.

We must transcend the duality of right and wrong, and have the courage to discover the brilliance of the Truth in everyone and everything. Truth can't be found in a simplistic set of rules of conduct, such as "If you do this, you will go to heaven, but if you break this law, you will go to hell." The commandments were made only to protect seekers in earlier stages from going astray.

Leaving this world without having killed a single mosquito or ant is no guarantee of high regard in the other world. If someone has killed mosquitoes but has also guided and saved thousands of people, rightness will be on that person's side. Rather than becoming good-natured cowards bound by commandments, we must have the courage to seek out and explore the rightness hidden deep within everyone and everything.

We are the captain and the crew who set sail on the ocean in search of the Truth. With the same spirit as Columbus, who put out to sea more than five hundred years ago and found a new continent, we are now sailing the ocean of Truth. No oceans or continents on earth remain undiscovered, so we must head for the world that lies beyond this one, the world of God—the Real World. Since science is essentially research into the unknown, exploring the spirit world is nothing less than the science of today and of the future—we are modern-day Magellans and Columbuses, Galileos and Copernicuses, scientists and explorers of the Truth. This spirit is the basis for Happy Science.

No Enlightenment without Self-Reflection

In chapter 1, "The Principle of Happiness," I explained the modern Fourfold Path of love, wisdom, self-reflection, and progress. By following the principles of happiness, you can explore and master these four paths. I have said repeatedly that the happiness we refer to is not a happiness we can enjoy only in this world *or* the other world, but a happiness that continues from this world to the next.

The way to true happiness is the way to enlightenment. When we attain enlightenment, we awaken to the Truth of our being, to the ideal way to live, and to knowing that we journey between this world and the other. Then, ultimately, we come to know that the world God created is a multidimensional world that extends from the three-dimensional world in which we are now experiencing spiritual refinement to the ninth dimension. Knowing leads to the attainment of enlightenment, and attaining enlightenment is happiness.

What great happiness, to know everything! No matter how lavish your lifestyle or how impressive your social status, unless you know where you have come from, where you are going, and how God views your life, you cannot savor true happiness. When we return to the other world, we cannot take our worldly status, reputation, or wealth with us. The only thing we can take to the other world is a pure and true mind. To ensure this, we must explore Right Mind and thoroughly learn the four principles of love, wisdom, self-reflection, and progress; these are the practical expressions of "rightness." They are the paths that incorporate the Theravada and Mahayana teachings, which we should follow to refine our souls.

In chapter 2, I discussed the principle of love. I explained that love is not only based on equality but involves different stages, and that there are different levels of love that you should strive to follow. Chapter 3 was on the principle of the mind, and focused on the exploration of Right Mind. In this chapter, "The Principle of Enlightenment," I explain the significance of self-reflection, the third principle of the Fourfold Path.

What is self-reflection? I said that knowing the Truth is the first step to attaining enlightenment. Human beings tend to take the easy way and live as they please, because they are content with the way they live. This being so, you need to look back on your life and see yourself objectively, examining yourself as if you were in a transparent glass box. To do this, you must have knowledge of the Truth. If you know how God's light unfolds, this knowledge becomes a light, or a mirror in which you will see yourself reflected. Start from knowing, and then the deep, deep quest for your inner self will begin.

Before your encounter with the Truth, did you ever reflect on your thoughts and deeds, or think about how to refine your thoughts? You may have been taught the importance of repentance at church or at home. But probably no one ever taught you that the principle of self-reflection is a way of exploring and finding your true nature as a child of God, or that it is a method of attaining enlightenment. Shakyamuni taught self-reflection twenty-six-hundred years ago in India.

After we are born into this world, most of us grow up in a family, are taught various things by our parents and schools, and are influenced by friends and society. As a consequence, for better or worse, we are tinted by different colors and live our lives unknowingly displaying these colors.[4] Everyone wants to lead a marvelous life, but many people trap themselves in grayness through their life choices. This is why we need to reflect on ourselves.

We did not come into this world clothed in dinginess; the original fabric of our minds was truly clean and pure. However, decades of living on earth leave our minds stained with different colors. Those whose minds are directed toward what is right are aglow with brilliant, heavenly colors, whereas those living wrongly are tinged with dark gray. Self-reflection launders the mind and rinses out dingy colors.

It is sad to see people who are ignorant of the distance they have moved from their original state of mind, and who are unaware of their estrangement from their own true nature. So the first step in self-reflection is to know the distance from God's mind to your own.

Advancement and Harmony

After we become aware of how far we still have to go, the next step is to come closer to our original state. Traditional Buddhism teaches various methods, such as the Noble Eightfold Path[5] and the Six Paramitas,[*6] but the basis of every method of enlightenment is two principles: advancement and harmony.

Advancement consists in achieving self-improvement and progress through individual efforts. Harmony means improving yourself without hurting others, and by contributing to the happiness of many. Just as

---

*The Six Paramitas is a teaching for attaining enlightenment through practicing and aiming for six perfections: giving, observing the precepts, patience, diligence, meditation, and wisdom.

trees grow, we grow in our understanding of the Truth. Trees that grow by harming other trees should be cut down. In order to be able to grow together, each tree must grow straight up toward the sky. If some trees grow at an angle, arching toward the ground or twisting, they impede the healthy growth of other trees. Each tree is allowed to grow but not at the cost of others, or conflict will arise. It is vital that while we progress we also aim for harmony.

What is behind these two principles of advancement and harmony? Every human being is a child of God, originating from the heart of God, so everyone is equal and of equal value. This equality is the origin of the principle of harmony.

The principle of advancement can be described as a principle of justice: although everyone starts out equal, people are impartially rewarded in response to their efforts.

For the universe to develop and prosper, the values both of progress and harmony—or justice and equality—must be realized.[7] Everyone has equal potential for limitless progress; however, the results will differ according to the effort each person makes. This is the way the world unfolds, and the Law that governs the universe encompasses both equality and justice.

Although everyone is a child of God, with the potential of infinite progress, some work hard and others do not. Some advance while others retreat. To reward everyone equally would be far from just. Think of the law of cause and effect,[8] action and reaction, which states that your results are a direct effect of your efforts—the more you put in, the more you get out, and vice versa. This applies equally to the principle of justice.

Shakyamuni believed in equality of spirit, and said that Buddha-nature is to be found in everyone and everything. He also clarified the concept of justice, teaching that there are different levels of enlightenment. Everything in this world is the result of the law of cause and effect. If someone is a natural leader but strays in the wrong direction, that person will suffer correspondingly. On the other hand, those who get started late will still receive God's blessings if they continue making a diligent effort and complete a considerable amount of work. These two principles are the basis of happiness and enlightenment.

If this is the case, we have only one direction in which to go. Every human being is a child of God and has an equal amount of divine nature, but everyone's divine nature is at a different level. We all must endeavor to love and respect the divine nature in each individual equally, no matter what its level, while at the same time striving to improve ourselves. This is the principle of enlightenment.

Remove the stains from your mind, restore it to its original brilliance, and refine your character. Then take a step forward to bring happiness to as many people as possible. Let us courageously take that first step toward further self-improvement.

FIVE

The Principle of
Progress

Self-Reflection as a Prerequisite for Progress

The progress taught at our organization is development through self-reflection. With this basis, progress and prosperity become secure and authentic.

We started our movement by establishing a strong footing, using the mottoes "First, build firm foundations" and "from the inside to the outside." These are not abstract notions; they embody the basic principles of our activities. Many people would like to create an ideal world, a utopia on earth—not only those who are involved in religion, but also those in politics, business, the arts, and cultural movements. Although they have their own ideals, they may not have their feet firmly on the ground. They attempt to save and lead others before they have built a strong inner self, which creates problems and confusion.

The idea of first establishing oneself is nothing new. The Chinese philosopher Confucius taught twenty-five hundred years ago[1] that in order to bring peace to the world, you need to cultivate yourself before you can govern your country. Shakyamuni Buddha taught the same idea: "First, refine yourself." Many of his disciples wanted to spread the Law as quickly as possible, but the Buddha restrained them, saying, "Do not be hasty. First refine the self. Keep on refining yourself throughout your life. There is no end to self-refinement. Know yourself and recognize where your weaknesses lie. When you preach to others, make sure that you are not arrogant. Never forget to reflect on yourself; it is when you forget to do this that you start to go astray."

Since Happy Science began, I've met and observed many members, listened to their opinions, and read their essays. The most difficult time for seekers of the Truth is when they start exercising their abilities and are beginning to be recognized by the world. Overconfidence is the first hurdle on the path to enlightenment. Unless you overcome this, you cannot continue on the path to enlightenment. Do not forget to reflect on yourself! Self-reflection curbs the human tendency to get over-excited and carried away by success.

Our goal is to awaken seven billion all over the world to the Truth, and to leave behind nourishment for the soul for future generations for two or even three thousand years to come. To keep from becoming content too easily, we must constantly remind ourselves that we have taken only the first step on the long path to our goal.

Some people may be highly advanced souls, but the more advanced you are, the more deeply you need to reflect on yourself. Do not become conceited or overly proud. Do not be too ready to regard yourself as a great figure. Always remind yourself that great figures must produce great results.

Progress through the Middle Way: The Infinite Evolution of Our Souls

Progress that happens through the Middle Way embraces infinite possibilities of evolution. This development never hurts yourself or others; it embraces infinite possibilities of evolution and progress.

Before you seek development, first you must avoid extremes and enter the Middle Way. Avoiding extremes doesn't mean stubbornly going straight ahead on a narrow path, no matter what happens. In the course of a life, you sometimes need to turn right or left. You can turn to the left or right when necessary, but unless you return to the center, you'll make mistakes.

You are not a robot, or a roller coaster that runs on a fixed track; you are an advanced soul who thinks and acts with free will. You are God's creation and have been endowed with the utmost freedom. Because you have such freedom, you need to adjust the course of your life so that you are always going in the right direction.

You can't spend your days meditating in a cave and avoiding contact with people. You live in society, so the challenge is to find ways that enable you to enter the Middle Way while still functioning in the world.

I mentioned that you must avoid extremes. One extreme is thinking and acting in a way that is clearly harmful to others. Take, for example, anger: How often do you get angry? Even highly respected religious leaders sometimes fly into rages when their pride is injured. These people do not yet know the real meaning of spiritual discipline; avoiding anger is the first stage of spiritual discipline for seekers of the Truth.

People usually get angry or upset because someone else has not acted according to their wishes, or as an automatic response to disappointment; this indicates that they are still at the most elementary stage of spiritual discipline. Since I awakened to spiritual Truth, I have never once become angry. I make an effort not only to understand other people's viewpoints, considering a situation from both their perspective and my own, but also to see it from the perspective of a neutral third person. I practice this in a split second, which prevents anger from engulfing my heart.

When you are overwhelmed by anger, you lose control of your mind and say harmful things that reflect only your own perspective. If, in that moment, you could consider the feelings of others, everything would be different. Moreover, if you could imagine that a third person was watching, such as the high spirits in heaven, for example, or God, you would discover yet another viewpoint. Once you make an immediate effort to see things from a different perspective, anger disappears; this is the first step of spiritual discipline.

Jealousy is another example of an emotion that harms others. Controlling jealousy is one of the keys to discipline for seekers. When you come across someone who seems to be more highly regarded than you, your pride is wounded. Why do you feel hurt? When you perceive someone is more highly valued or loved than you, you instantly feel less loved. It is a lack of love that makes you feel sad and sets flames of jealousy burning in your heart.

However, you must strive to change this pattern of thinking because jealousy harms you as much as it harms others. Everyone has an ideal image of the self deep within, an image of the idealized self. The truth is that someone you are jealous of actually embodies your ideal image of yourself. Deep down, you wish you could be like that person, but because you are not, you can't bear that person occupying the place you feel is rightfully yours.

Jealousy ultimately damages the ideal you have of yourself. At a subconscious level, it stops you coming closer to your own ideal image and moves you in the opposite direction.

Those who are jealous tend to attribute the cause of their problem to others instead of reflecting on themselves. However, the cause of the problem lies in their lack of generosity in accepting others who are held in higher regard. They have no real confidence in themselves. These people know only too well that they've achieved nothing worthy of others' recognition, yet they still want to be praised. There is a gap between their ideal and the reality.

To close this gap, many try to draw public attention to themselves; for example, they appear on television or get famous and become the center of attention. Others try to close the gap by becoming spiritual leaders. People who choose this option have already given up on worldly success but still hope to stand in the spotlight of a spiritual group and gain respect. Some of them have actually come to our group, wanting to be recognized as great spiritual leaders.

These people must first reflect on the cause of their jealousy. If they were confident of their own worth, they wouldn't care what other people say, but they are empty inside and are trying to compensate for this emptiness. What should these people do? One way to build confidence is to continue diligently with spiritual discipline, day after day. Daily effort is very important. You cannot expect to overcome a sense of inferiority or erase negative feelings instantly with superficial success. In the midst of praise or censure from others, you need to hold on to your unshakable self and observe yourself calmly.

Starting from the Ordinary

Many people are gifted. You may know someone in your office who seems to be without faults, someone whose conversation is clever and witty, who is an efficient worker, athletic, and multitalented. There is usually one person like this in every workplace, someone who always exhibits great talent and arouses the envy of others. In the presence of such a person, you may actually feel a sense of inferiority.

I worked with a man like this. At first I felt envious of his abilities, but after a while I came to realize that he was always trying his hardest to impress, and never felt at ease unless people were saying, "He is incredible." At heart, he was lonely. People like this crave meaningful recognition. They think that if they appear to be superior and multitalented, they will be recognized.

I got to know this colleague, but something insincere about him made him not very likable. This sort of person hates to reveal the slightest weakness or show others any part of himself he feels is inferior, so he tries to protect himself with a hard shell. As a result, his mind is always turbulent, full of anxiety and irritation.

While it is important to have a broad perspective and a wide range of experience, those who are good at everything seem to lead rather lonely lives. Although their lives may look wonderful to others, they are not necessarily personally fulfilling. Everyone else may applaud their lives, but they themselves are not satisfied. Seeing this, I wanted to lead a life that I could be happy with, not a life that everyone else admired.

At a certain point, it may be important to be able to give up some abilities. You might feel disappointed hearing me say this in a chapter on progress, but what leads to development is your awareness of being ordinary. Everyone is given just twenty-four hours each day; it is the same for you and me, and for everyone else in this world. People rarely live for more than a hundred years. When you get up each morning, you have twenty-four hours in your hands; everyone lives within this framework. As long as we live within these limitations, we cannot hope to become all-knowing geniuses who excel in every subject.

There have been geniuses such as Leonardo da Vinci, but very few people can live as he did. We have to start with the awareness that we are ordinary people. You may wonder if you were a great angel of light in a past life, but although this thought might be useful for inspiring enthusiasm, it is important to start with an awareness of being ordinary. Only when you start from the ordinary will you come to appreciate steady advancement in your life.

A Modern Interpretation of the Middle Way

The 80/20 Percent Approach

Unless you concentrate on what truly resonates with your soul and accords with your inner ideals, you will waste a lot of time and energy in your life. This isn't a problem if you have unlimited talent, but for most people it is essential to prioritize their limited resource of time. This is the key to successful living.

I used to work for a trading company, and while there, I was careful not to become totally absorbed in unimportant matters. In my last few years at the trading company, my main interest was spiritual studies, so I decided on a policy of putting 80 percent of my energy into the study of the Truth and the remaining 20 percent into gaining worldly experience. I used 20 percent of my energy to experience things I could not have experienced in a world apart from society.

A trading company employee in Japan usually plays golf once a month, for either business or pleasure, and I was not exempt from this social obligation. However, I never became absorbed in it—it was a question of compromise. Because I wasn't interested enough to advance much beyond beginner level, I didn't need to spend much time practicing.

The same applied to other sports. In high school, I practiced kendo, a Japanese martial art, and reached quite a high level. In university, practice could have taken me to an even higher level, but when I saw how much time kendo would take away from my other activities, I decided not to spend any more time on it. I played tennis, too, and was the captain of the company tennis team, but again did not become deeply involved.

I've done many other things, but my basic policy has been to compromise and just attain a reasonable level. I've never felt the need to be good at everything, but I've been sociable enough to get on well with other people. I dedicated 80 percent of my energy to my vocation and 20 percent to other experiences, but I never got intensely involved in activities I didn't find particularly meaningful. It is crucially important to hold fast to what is essential.

Once you grasp the essential, you are on your way to boundless success. This is because it's possible to make a constant effort to achieve what you find worthwhile, tirelessly devoting yourself to something for five, ten, or twenty years. On the other hand, you can't keep doing something that doesn't have meaning for you.

If you have been born into this world with a limited number of abilities, you must not give up searching for the part of your soul that is the most gifted, the most attractive, the most wonderful. You must endeavor to draw out what is best in you. If there are only twenty-four hours in a day, make the most of these hours in order to live the best possible life. This is one practical application of the Middle Way for contemporary times.

Seekers of the Truth cannot function in this world with no interest in anything other than the Truth. You might be able to protect your inner kingdom* by concentrating only on the Truth, but you will have no opportunity to be influenced by people you meet, or to influence them. I don't expect you to live in seclusion like a philosopher; if you wanted to live that way, you should have stayed in the heavenly realm. Yet you decided to be born into this world, which means you have decided to nourish your soul through relationships with others.

The more you refine yourself, the greater the influence you will have on others. Even in experiences that seem like a waste of time, strive to find the gem that will refine your soul. It is silly to spend 100 percent of your time on things that don't interest you, but it's also not right to spend 100 percent of your time devoted to your own interests, because you'll miss the opportunity to have an influence on others.

I give lectures regularly, but I'd like to talk to even more people. However, the idea of the Middle Way applies to my lifestyle, too. I do not live solely for myself or solely for others. I have enough time for myself, but I always like to have opportunities to meet and influence as many people as possible, and to be influenced by them.

I spend 80 percent of my time refining myself and the remaining 20 percent meeting people. Perhaps this ratio seems strange to you. You might think that if I really wished to convey the Truth to, and save, as many people as possible, I should spend twenty-four hours a day meeting people. However, the idea of spending all of one's time meeting people is like a sprinter versus a marathoner. You may be able to run a hundred yards at top speed, but at that pace you won't be able to finish the long-distance marathon of life. First make your own foothold strong, and then make it your aim to have gradual influence on others.

---

*Everyone has free will and is given complete autonomy to govern his or her own mind. Utopia begins within the mind of each individual, when that person manages to control the mind and maintain a state of peace.

Accumulating Knowledge and Wisdom
beneath the Surface

It is important to put aside time for planning and preparing for the future and not expend all your time and energy on the present. I practice this strategy because I teach the Truth. No matter how diligently I study the human mind, I can never study enough.

You may be filled with enthusiasm and passion for conveying the joy of knowing the Truth to as many people as possible, but you must not forget to accumulate inner strength and recharge yourself. If you neglect to do this, you will be easily swayed by your relationships with others. If you expose 100 percent of yourself to others, you can be shaken and influenced by other people's opinions of you. Instead, aim to reveal only 10 to 20 percent of yourself to others, like the tip of an iceberg; the other 80 to 90 percent should remain deep beneath the surface. Only when there is a part of you below the surface that remains steady can you withstand the rough waves of life. If the part above the surface is your entire being, you can be buffeted from one extreme to another. Don't be too concerned with what is above the surface. Rather, have confidence in the part of yourself that lies beneath the surface and is not readily apparent.

How much of you lies in reserve, below the surface? When you take away the part that is exposed, the part that others praise, what remains? What remains after your job or your family drops away? If you remove the parts of you that others praise, what is left? The larger the base hidden underwater becomes, the more stable the iceberg; it will not be swayed by rough waves. In this way you will develop an unshakable mind.

Building the self beneath the surface is also a method of entering the Middle Way. If you reveal almost all of your being to others and don't have confidence in the parts you have revealed, you will get angry, jealous, and resentful about negative remarks they may make. If, on the other hand, you are absolutely confident of the 80 to 90 percent of you that remains hidden, you will not become emotional or hostile in the face of criticism. You get emotional simply because you cling to your ego and think only of yourself. If you really care about yourself, cultivate and expand your deeper self.

I said earlier that one method of entering the Middle Way is to expend 80 percent of your energy on the areas that most interest you and 20 percent on a variety of other experiences. In other words, you should develop the part of the iceberg that is below the water in order to stabilize your life and guide you to the Middle Way. It is important that you build a firm foundation for your life. With this, you will be able to withstand whatever winds and waves you encounter.

Always Moving Forward

The third method of entering the Middle Way is to continually move forward. When you first tried to ride a bicycle, you probably wondered how on earth people could ride such an unstable vehicle. You may have thought, "How can I possibly not fall over when there are only two thin wheels? For a vehicle to be stable, usually there have to be four wheels, or at least three, yet someone invented this and somehow people are actually able to ride it."

A bicycle falls over as soon as it stops, but as long as it's moving, it's fine. Herein lies the secret: in order to stay balanced and realize your ideals while walking the Middle Way, you need to keep on moving forward. Only when you are steadily moving forward can you avoid going to extremes and enter the Middle Way. Entering the Middle Way doesn't mean sitting still and doing nothing. The Middle Way is a path on which to move and make progress.

Self-Reflection as a Method of Entering the Middle Way

The True Meaning of Self-Reflection

There are three necessary components for entering the Middle Way: The first is to allocate 80 percent of your time and energy to your main interests, the second is to build a firm base beneath the surface, and the third is to keep moving forward.

There is also a more traditional means of entering the Middle Way: self-reflection. When you reflect on yourself, you need to know that deep within you is the true self that shines brilliantly, like a diamond. Reflecting on yourself doesn't mean focusing only on your faults or correcting the mistakes you've made, based on the assumption that human beings are born sinful. Rather, it means using various methods and checkpoints to find the shining self deep within you. Do not forget that your essential nature is part of God, and that you are connected to him. There is a golden pipeline within through which light flows from higher spirits directly into you.

First, understand that deep within, your nature is wonderful and radiant. Then, knowing that, strive to remove the dirt that is clogging the pipe. After practicing self-reflection, you should start radiating light. If you see only your shortcomings and feel miserable, you haven't found your true essence as a child of God.

You will need careful one-on-one instruction, but the goal of self-reflection is not to make you feel sinful or miserable. Through self-reflection, I expect you to feel clean and light, as you do when dirt has been washed from your physical body. You need to recognize that you are truly warm, clear-minded, kind, and marvelous.

One of the methods for removing this dirt is through the Noble Eightfold Path.

Right View

First comes Right View, or seeing things rightly. But the act of "seeing" is not a simple thing. You see yourself and others in a certain way and other people see you and others differently. However, you may live for years without being aware of this gap in perception. A person may have the self-perception of being worthless despite the praise of others. This person does not see rightly. On the other hand, someone else may overestimate his abilities and be quite unaware of other people's critical views.

When you identify only with what the physical eyes see, your viewpoint becomes inflexible.

Try to look at things from a perspective outside of yourself.

Overestimating your abilities makes you arrogant, but underestimating yourself is also wrong. It is essential to see yourself rightly. To see yourself rightly, you need to understand many different viewpoints and maintain balanced self-perception. Even if someone speaks ill of you, there will be others who value you highly. Balanced thinking functions as a safety net in your life.

The human tendency is to adopt an all-or-nothing attitude, and we tend to go to extremes by thinking we are either totally loved or totally hated. However, it is impossible for someone to hate you completely or like you completely.

Right Thought

The Noble Eightfold Path also includes the practice of Right Thought. This is difficult, but very basic. Many people are not aware that what they think actually determines who they are. They identify themselves with their social status, the name on their driver's license, the school they graduated from, or the company for which they work. Some identify with the approving remarks of others. However, none of these is correct.

The Roman philosopher-emperor Marcus Aurelius wrote in *Meditations* that one's thoughts reveal who one is. More recently, the American poet and philosopher Ralph Waldo Emerson explored this idea. The field of psychology uses this concept to help people struggling in this world, and indeed it is the truth. In the other world, where everyone goes after death, there is nothing but thought; what you actually think is who you are. In the other world, if you feel you have a physical body, it is because you imagine you have one; essentially, physical attributes such as arms, legs, mouths, and even brains do not exist. Thought is the only thing that exists there. Your thoughts determine everything.

Through the eternal cycle of reincarnation,* we refine our thinking. If you understand Right Thought, you can complete about 80 percent of your spiritual discipline in this lifetime. However, most people do not give serious consideration to their thoughts, nor are they even aware that they are actually thinking. They live each day without paying any attention to the importance of thinking, and only fragments of thoughts pass randomly through their heads. For example, they think about what they will eat for lunch, after a meal they think they feel sleepy, or they think they need some coffee to wake them up. If only random thoughts wander through your head, it indicates that you don't really understand what thinking is.

In a day, you have at least sixteen hours in which to think. Have you ever reflected on these thoughts? What has been in your mind for those sixteen hours? Nothing? Some emotions? Your thoughts may be stuck on one particular concern, such as money, your family, your job or boss, and you may spend all your time worrying about it. Is it all right to waste your time like that? If your thoughts are the most important thing, is it all right simply to let them come and go?

Examining your thoughts is an important part of the practice of self-reflection. Each day you need to set aside some time to examine the thoughts you have had during that day; through this practice you discover your real state. If you find your sixteen hours have been filled with high-minded thoughts, your soul is actually highly refined. If your thoughts have been filled with love and compassion, you are quite exceptional. If you look back on your thoughts through the day and find they were clouded, it means your soul is not yet purified.

But once again, you should not adopt an all-or-nothing attitude. It is almost impossible to think only good thoughts. In any given day, you probably think both good and bad thoughts. But whenever you think negative thoughts, it is important to dismiss them and steer your thoughts back in the right direction.

---

*The souls of human beings are given eternal life and undergo repeated incarnations, coming into this world from the other world in order to refine and improve themselves.

Very few people can think only positive thoughts, so always examine your thoughts as if they were in a transparent glass box. Although it may be difficult, you can correct the negative thoughts that come up, and that will purify your mind. Once you understand this process, it is essential to practice it every day.

Self-Reflection Leads to Progress

In this chapter on the principle of progress, the focus is on spiritual development through the Middle Way. This is closely related to Right Effort and Right Mindfulness, which are part of the Noble Eightfold Path.

Right Effort

I have previously emphasized the importance of making an effort. Even if you start out as an ordinary person, through constant daily effort you will be able to unfold a brilliant future. No matter how slow or unremarkable you may be, through accumulated effort you will be able to achieve greatness in the future.

There are many people who possess wonderful abilities, talents, and intelligence, and in a matter of a year or two they acquire expertise in a particular field. If you are ordinary, you can aim to achieve the same in five or ten years. I don't envy those who are talented and can master things in a shorter time, because I know I can undoubtedly reach the same level if I work five or ten times longer. Besides, that means I can enjoy the process of getting to the goal for that much longer.

If you think you are not especially clever, be thankful that you have an opportunity to study that much more. If you are aware that you are ordinary, achievement will bring you all the more joy. So the less able you feel, the deeper your gratitude should be; you have much potential that will bloom through continuous effort. This is one way of understanding the path of Right Effort.

Right Mindfulness

Right Mindfulness means using the power of the will in the right way, which is closely connected to self-realization. Depending on how you hold to your ideals and how you realize them, your will can either cause problems or be the key to your success in life.

Nowadays, self-realization is a popular theme; you may already be studying it through books or seminars. However, the aim of most theories of self-realization seems to be winning the admiration of others or achieving worldly success. The new set of values that Happy Science encourages embodies the perspective of God and high spirits. If you have some knowledge of the Truth, aim for true self-realization that accords with God's ideals, rather than superficial worldly success. Remember this whenever you aim to achieve something.

More and more people are joining our organization, and many of them say that they want to do something to help us in our work of conveying the Truth. I appreciate their enthusiasm and high ideals, but sometimes they are slightly misguided. Conveying the Truth must be for the sake of God, not to fulfill personal desires. The starting point is always that we are volunteers aiming to realize God's ideals.

I started this movement to realize God's ideals, not my own personal goals. It is good to have high ideals, but when you pursue them, do not do so from a mistaken perspective. Do not take advantage of this movement for your own self-realization, or to make a name for yourself in this world. God's ideals come first; then we, as part of a great river, flow toward his ideals. Never forget your role as a single drop of water in this river.

Right Mindfulness, or maintaining a strong will, is one of the principles of success and development.[2] But always remember that the ultimate goal of true development must be God's mind, and that his mind represents the ultimate development of love.

Love, Prayer, and Self-Realization

When you aim to realize an ideal, prayer is important. Prayer can be used to achieve true development. However, your prayers should not be only for your own happiness; rather, you should pray to come closer to God's ideals, the ultimate ideals, and to be able to work in a way that will help him. Do not ever mistake the reason you pray; in your prayers, ask the high spirits to lead you to serve God with devotion.

Strive for true self-realization and true success by practicing love and prayer in the right way. God is the ultimate development of love. We all live in the flow of a great river of love, and are moving steadily toward him. Love is everything: life, light, and energy. This awareness is the basis for praying to realize great ideals.

Above all else, make a constant effort to reflect on yourself, to build a strong self, and to enter the Middle Way. Through this effort, boundless love and prayer will be attained and a path to true success will unfold before you. Let us walk the path that leads to true success together.

SIX

The Principle of Wisdom

The Basis of Learning

Since establishing Happy Science, I have been busy managing it, listening to member concerns, considering the problems my readers write to me about, and exploring and expounding the Laws. Not only have I been teaching, but I've also been given the opportunity to learn a lot from others.

Wisdom is the third principle of happiness, and I have been speaking and writing about the many forms it takes. There are different levels of refinement and different scales of wisdom, and they produce different effects.

I've spent a great deal of time studying the theme of wisdom, and have established the theory of the developmental stages of wisdom, which I will discuss later. Intellectual inquiry has long been one of my main interests. Whenever I look within, I always feel a strong desire to improve myself, and I have long contemplated how to harness this burning enthusiasm. For years I searched for answers in various philosophies and ways of approaching life. During that time I began to perceive wisdom as the result of my own experiences, and my experiences are reflected in the teaching methods at Happy Science.

Spiritual discipline is not found simply by sitting on a mountaintop and meditating, or by obsessing over a desire for supernatural abilities. So how should seekers of Truth refine their souls without renouncing the world? To find a method, we need to consider the ways in which wisdom relates to spiritual discipline.

In our world, knowledge is highly valued in every walk of life. However, there is a tendency to be concerned only with the style and framework of knowledge, without understanding its true essence.[1] Through my years of study, I have come to understand what lies beyond knowledge, and I have found a method of spiritual discipline that is safe and appropriate for broad use.

If you merely explore and gather knowledge that other people have already discovered and presented, you cannot know the true blessing that knowledge can bring. If you go beyond received wisdom and break through to the utmost depths of the human mind, you find the source of human wisdom.[2] Once you have reached this wellspring, you feel an infinite power welling up from within. The power of the wisdom that gushes from the depths of this spring enables you to solve any difficulty in life, like a great sword cutting through a Gordian knot.*

From thousands of letters from all over the world, it seems clear that many people don't understand the exact nature of the difficulties they face, nor do they know how to solve them, much less how to transform them into something better, or higher, that will lead them to happiness. I've realized how important it is to have a strong intellectual foundation—a breadth of inner knowledge—and this realization has led me to develop the current methods of teaching at Happy Science.

I had a yearning for wisdom that started to reveal itself when I was nineteen or twenty, like an inexhaustible spring that was continuously streaming forth from deep within me. In my youth, I always had two overwhelming passions—a passion for learning and a passion to use this learning for a higher purpose. I did not know my mission or my future

---

*In 1579, Gordius, the king of Phrygia, tied a knot so intricate that it could be untied only by the future ruler of Asia. Alexander the Great cut it with his sword.

work, so while under the sway of these passions, I devoted all of my energy to developing myself intellectually.

Looking back at those years, I realize that many of the books I chose to read contained the words and thoughts of high spirits who later sent me spiritual messages. I chose them naturally and instinctively, like a salmon swimming upstream, back to its birthplace. In those times, one of my guiding basic principles was "Do not be satisfied until you are fully convinced." I never felt I had understood something until I became convinced of it in the deepest recesses of my mind. Until I had digested it completely, I never stopped studying it or felt satisfied with my conclusions.

I explored many different fields of thought and study. I delved into literature, the fine arts, science, philosophy, religion, poetry, business management, law, politics, economics, and international affairs. I searched continuously and assiduously for the great wisdom of humankind, which continues to sparkle like a diamond despite the passage of time.

I thought of remaining at university and becoming an academic, but rejected that path because I was dissatisfied with academic studies alone. The academic world today seems to have its own set of rules, and scholars do their research only within the framework of those rules. In the academic world, analysis and objectivity are highly valued, and the academic approach of Max Weber still dominates the mainstream in modern research. Indeed, before presenting original thought, one must investigate, quote, and document relevant ideas already put forward by others.

As I observed the existing academic system, I realized that it was like a world inside a kaleidoscope. It appears magical and beautiful, but beyond its surface appearance the magical world is simply bits of paper, and not real. Since I maintained the attitude of exploring everything until I became fully convinced of its validity and was able to understand it deeply, most current academic studies began to fade from my vision.

My many books on spiritual matters contain very few background references. I have revealed only what I myself have investigated, pondered, and practiced until I gained a complete understanding. All the ideas in my books struck a chord in my heart and radiated a bright light within me. This brilliant light is the self-reflection of my inner light and my own thoughts. I never talked about, or published, anything that I did not feel I was wholly convinced of or completely understood. This was the starting point of Happy Science.

In my current lectures and books, I still continue to hold to the policy of never revealing more than 10 percent of what I have learned. I believe I must hold back the other 90 percent in order to maintain credibility, so the more books I write and the more lectures I give, the more study and contemplation I need to do. Only what we grasp through our heart, not merely with our brain, becomes true nourishment for the soul.*

There is a great deal to see and hear in this life, but in time, much of it will pass and fade. A huge amount of information is produced every day, but in the end, most of it will simply disappear without a trace. When you finally leave this world, you can take with you only what has reached the very core of your soul. This is what forms your character.

Many people live and work in the world of knowledge, but few study what is below the surface. Unless you penetrate the surface and grasp the true meaning of what lies beneath the words, you cannot gain real power, nor can you take that knowledge with you to the other world.

This is true for writings in any tongue, be it Japanese, English, or any other language. When I read books written in a foreign language, some are written in a way that deeply touches my heart, while others don't move me at all. Although English is not my native language, there are writings in English that touch me profoundly. The writers use words that stand the test of time, words that have been part of the English language for centuries. This is why their works inspire even readers who are not native English speakers.

---

*This nourishment for the soul is the knowledge and experiences essential to its development.

I have published many books written in simple Japanese that touch the hearts of my readers. Although the contents are of a higher order, these books are written very plainly, using words that have withstood the test of time and are proven to have "spirit." There is much wisdom in my writings, but the style is simple. I can write in this way because I have never deceived myself. I explore everything thoroughly until I am convinced of its validity, and can express my understanding in an easy, natural way.

The words of those who lack this depth of wisdom are just a show of vanity, a meaningless flow of phrases. Bookstores are flooded with uninspiring books written by authors interested only in the superficial meaning of words or the neat arrangement of words as symbols. These authors have not reached the depths of language or found the spirit of words.

I accept only that which I fully understand, and I make this policy the foundation of my intellectual life. You are able to study using my lectures, but I couldn't do that, because I could rarely accept or completely agree with what other lecturers said. If a speaker had pursued the Truth in the same way that I did, his mind and my mind would have resonated in harmony, but this rarely happened. For this reason, I worked hard to develop my own teachings.

Famous works of literature that are accepted masterpieces can be ranked according to the level of Truth they embody, but many people cannot differentiate the different levels of Truth. Some masterpieces have actually been written by angels of light, while other works are attuned to the vibrations of hell. Yet all are regarded as top-class writing. Literary works are generally evaluated by their story line and style, but we must discover what exists beyond superficial technique.

I have read many novels, and I suppose their authors are revealing their own ideas, just as I am doing now. This makes them responsible for whether or not their work attracts interest, enlightens others, and withstands the test of time. If authors don't consider these points, their work is only worth reading to pass the time of day. When you read a book, you need to look carefully for what is behind the mass of words and get beyond all the gilding to discover the essence of a writer's message.

This applies not only to literature, but also to academic studies. You have to get beyond vanity, embellishment, conventions, and rules in order to find the essence of the thinker's message. The question is whether the core concept of a book, if summarized in one page, contains Truth. No matter how many books an author has written, if the core message is wrong, they are of absolutely no value.

At Happy Science, we have many different seminars and tests to encourage spiritual progress, and I've read numerous essays written by members. The poor quality of the essays written by those in professions requiring intellectual ability often surprises me; many of these people are too concerned with their writing skills to say honestly what they think. I always ask members to express what they have discovered, what they truly understand, and what they really want to say in plain language that even children could grasp. But usually people cannot write this way; they haven't gone deeply enough into their inner world or confronted themselves seriously.

If you sincerely wish to pursue wisdom, you need to be honest with yourself. Drop all pretense and vanity, then confront the ideas of others head on and draw your own conclusions. In the process, you will meet many people, hear many arguments, and encounter many problems, all testing the strength of your convictions. If your thoughts are no more than vanity, they will be blown away like dust in the wind. But if your thoughts are firmly rooted and come from deep within, they will be unshakable. Through various experiences, your thoughts will gradually develop an increasing brilliance.

So if you wish to gain deep and lasting wisdom, first open your heart. If you explore wisdom merely out of a desire to look good in the eyes of others, knowledge will lead you into a labyrinth. As long as you continue to study in this way, although you may come to the belief that you have found greatness and enlightenment, you will be mistaken. As you study many hours a day and accumulate knowledge, check to see whether you can explain what you have learned in plain language.

If you have truly understood a book of Truth, you will be able to explain the contents briefly, in simple words. If you cannot, it means that you haven't yet understood it. When you can speak freely on a theme for five brief minutes or ten long hours, then you can say you have really understood what a book is about.

If you continue reading with this understanding, it will no longer matter to you who said what or in which book. Only essential wisdom that radiates light will remain in your soul, like the gold dust left in a sifting pan. Continuously try to grasp the very core of a thought. Discover what you truly agree with in the depths of your heart. This effort will create and develop the part of your soul that truly shines. This is the basis of learning.

Acquiring Higher Awareness

The Significance of Intellectual Pursuits

Learning is closely connected to the reason we have been given eternal life. First, realize that God values learning, and has given it to us as a tool for our development. If learning were meaningless, then the fact that we reincarnate again and again over thousands, tens of thousands, or even millions of years would be without meaning.

So, what significance does God attach to learning? The secret lies in the fact that each one of us is a unique individual. Each individual is an artistic creation of light, brilliant and multihued like a rainbow after the rain. There is a supreme being who deems it wonderful to create this artistic diversity of light. Each individual soul is expected to use its own tendencies and personality for learning.

Why are we required to learn so much? Why is learning considered so good? We need to consider this question in the context of everyday life. Why are you reading this book? Can you come up with a clear answer? Whether or not you can is important.

Everyone is given certain problems to solve in individual unique circumstances, and you have to solve these issues on your own. You may find people who will give you advice, but in the end, no one but you can solve your problems. No doubt you have worries and challenges that you are trying to solve and use as a springboard for further development in your life. Perhaps you expect to find some clues about how to solve your problems in my book.

Each person is given a unique workbook of life problems to solve. We must unravel our problems on our own, but we get helpful ideas from people who are living, as well as from the writings of those now passed. People are always looking for information about how to lead a better life, and although God expects us to complete our workbook on our own, he still provides clues. We can also meet people who become our teachers, or who at least give us clues at propitious moments; this might happen at home or elsewhere. Finding clues to help us solve our problems is the starting point of learning.

What Is Awareness?

What will happen once we have the clues to help us solve the problems in our life? What will the result be of collecting these clues? If they do nothing but confuse you, they are useless.

The goal of learning is higher awareness. The secret to living happily and enjoying developing through high ideals is having a higher awareness, or a higher perspective. Having a higher awareness means you have the key to solve the various problems in your life. It is generally easy for you to find solutions to the problems that young children face, but it is more difficult to help solve the problems of those in situations similar to your own, because there is no difference between your level of awareness and theirs.

People who have a higher perspective can easily solve the problems of those who haven't yet reached that level; this is the reason people seek a teacher who has a higher understanding. Someone trapped in a whirlpool of suffering, engaged in a life-and-death struggle, is generally unable to see the cause of such trouble. Those regarded as teachers have a higher level of awareness, and can both understand the causes of a problem and use past examples to help resolve it. Those who see things according to the law of cause and effect can swiftly point out why someone is unable to escape from suffering.

I have heard that hens are easily captive to their own imagination. Once a hen has been tethered with a rope and then freed, anything long that looks like a rope, even a line drawn with chalk, will immobilize the hen, because she thinks she has been tied up again. Due to a low level of awareness, a hen becomes paralyzed by her own imagination and actually cannot move, bound by restraining memories of the past. We feel pity for the hen, but there is a huge difference between her level of awareness and that of a human being.

There is a similar story from Algeria about how to catch a monkey with a coconut. You make a hole in the coconut just big enough for the monkey's hand to fit through, then you scoop out the inside, put in some rice, and hang it from a tree. The monkey will plunge its hand into the coconut and try to grab the rice inside. Once it grabs the rice, it won't be able to pull out its closed fist. If it lets go of the rice, it can be free, but the monkey doesn't have a high enough level of awareness to understand that. The monkey only knows that it is trapped and has no idea of how to escape. It struggles desperately to get free but doesn't think of releasing the rice, and so is easily caught. The monkey doesn't have sufficient awareness to be able to reconcile two desires: wanting the rice and wanting to escape.

Imagine yourself in the same situation. If you put your hand through the hole in the coconut to grab some rice and couldn't take your fist out, you would immediately understand that it was because your fist was bigger than the hole. You would instantly be aware that if you let go of the rice, you would be free. However, with its limited awareness, the monkey falls into a life-threatening trap. It just wants food and simply tries to take it, but, unable to escape, suffers in agony until dawn.

This is how we on earth appear to the high spirits in heaven. We often suffer over such small things, just like this poor monkey, unable to find solutions because we cannot see the real cause of our problems. As a result we become overwhelmed, at a complete loss as to what to do.

There is a French philosopher, Alain,* who is aware of some important Truths. Here are a few examples from his book, *On Happiness*.

A baby keeps crying loudly, and no one knows what to do. The baby's parents wonder what is wrong, whether the baby wants milk, is too cold or too hot, or is sick, and eventually they take the baby to the doctor. The doctor finds nothing wrong with the infant and the parents are at a complete loss. The cause of the problem turns out to be very simple—an open safety pin in the baby's sweater. The baby is crying because the pin is causing pain, but unaware of this, the adults imagine many different possible causes.

Another parable took place in the ancient kingdom of Macedonia, Greece, where there was an unruly horse that no one could ride. People didn't understand the horse's unease, so they thought it was violent by nature and impossible to control, and looked for someone brave enough to train it. Although it was considered a difficult challenge, one man succeeded quite easily. He alone was able to see that the horse was violent because it was afraid of its own shadow. The problem was the horse's habit of looking down and seeing its shadow, not knowing what it was and being frightened by it. The more furiously the horse struggled, the more crazily its shadow danced, creating strange, terrifying patterns. When the man pulled the reins so tight that the horse could no longer see its shadow, it calmed down. The solution was not to remove the shadow, but simply to keep the horse from seeing it.

As Alain illustrates in these stories, most difficulties in life have their origin in an inability to see the fundamental cause of a problem.

---

*Alain (1868–1951) is the pseudonym of Émile-Auguste Chartier, French philosopher and essayist.

The cause can be unexpectedly simple, like a pin in a sweater or being afraid of shadows. Seemingly great difficulties, whether they involve finance, business, health, or family, may also have simple causes. Because we don't realize this, we become trapped and confused.

First we must find the "pin" or the "shadow" in our problem. To do this, we need to step back from any fixed ideas and see the problem from a higher perspective. Then we will discover our blind spots. A higher awareness is essential in doing this, and you can gain it through learning.

Those who have learned much in past incarnations have a higher level of awareness. Someone of a higher spiritual level has a higher awareness, with a better understanding of the feelings and worries of a greater number of people and an ability to help them solve their problems. No matter how many books you read, unless you gain a higher awareness through reading them, you won't understand these things. Those who have gathered clues to help solve life's problems, digested them, and formed their own thoughts and ideas can instantly understand the worries of others and help to solve them. The basic purpose of learning is to acquire a higher level of awareness. You need to acquire the ability to see instantly that a baby is crying because a pin is pricking it, not because it wants milk or is sick; or to see that a horse is not violent by nature, but simply afraid of its own shadow.

Acquiring a Higher Awareness

As we confront our own problems in life, we must never stop making a constant effort to acquire a higher awareness.[3] That is why we need to study a wide variety of different subjects.

One of the reasons for my many books is to provide you with as much material as possible to increase your awareness. In reading the high-level thoughts of learned men and women, sometimes you can easily find solutions to your problems. Such collections of thoughts are guidebooks that assist you in solving the problems you face in life. We need to use every experience and all our knowledge to raise our level of awareness; this is precisely the objective of our spiritual refinement on earth.

I teach that the spirit world is composed of different stages or dimensions: the fourth, fifth, sixth, seventh, eighth, and ninth dimensions. The difference between these dimensions lies not in a person's status or reputation, but in the level of awareness. The higher the awareness we attain, the broader the perspective with which we see the world, and the deeper our understanding of others and of the will of God. Reincarnation gives us the ability to have even more experiences that serve to increase our understanding.

When you face difficult problems or situations, the wisest approach is to try to discover a new source of awareness. You need to make an effort to understand your own tendencies clearly, to understand the way you think about a particular situation. Try to find a solution much more quickly the next time you face a similar problem. If it took you a week to solve a certain problem, next time make an effort to solve it in a day, an hour, a minute, or even a second.

Effort is the driving force behind the development of human culture. Culture is created through the accumulation of human effort. Without the cumulative achievements of humanity, there would be no basis for the creation of new culture by the generations that follow. Development is based on the culture left by those who have come before, so culture can be said to be an accumulation of human awareness.

Let me repeat the two main points I've made so far. First, never deceive yourself about learning; be honest and unaffected, and continue to explore until you become truly convinced of an idea. This attitude is the basis of learning.

Second, the main objective of learning is to acquire a higher level of awareness. From this perspective, you will be able to understand the significance of spiritual refinement on earth. When you face life's difficulties, don't become discouraged or depleted; rather, learn new lessons continually so that you become able to see the "pin" or the "shadow" in a problem instantly, and raise your level of awareness by one or two degrees.

The Developmental Stages of Wisdom

In chapter 2, I explained that there are developmental stages of love. There are also stages of wisdom. Those who have already advanced to higher stages of wisdom can easily comprehend that there are different stages, but those who have not yet reached these levels cannot easily understand this concept.

The Period of Intellectual Struggle

The first stage of wisdom is collecting information and tools that increase your awareness. It is essential to attain as much knowledge as possible, including the thoughts of those who are more advanced than you. If you do not pass through this stage, you will be easily swayed by the opinions of others, and every time you encounter a problem, you'll be at a loss as to what to do. However, those who have struggled to establish themselves in this first stage can use their knowledge and experience to build and increase their awareness. With a higher level of awareness, they can quite easily solve most of the usual problems that keep ordinary people worrying for years. So the benefits that accrue even at this stage are considerable.

In the business world, too, many executives devote a great deal of energy to becoming established in this first stage of wisdom. Top managers can instantly find solutions to problems that their subordinates struggle with and find impossible to solve. This ability is sometimes described simply as inspiration, but a certain intellectual effort is required before you start receiving inspiration. You must continue to learn, absorb higher knowledge, and gain the confidence to know when you have assimilated sufficient knowledge. This self-confidence is essential in becoming established in the first stage of wisdom.

This first stage of wisdom leads to sensing the existence of the spirit world. Through studying the works of a variety of thinkers, then deepening that knowledge further and further in my own mind, I became able to receive more inspiration. Now my spiritual heart has opened,* and I am able to communicate at will with inhabitants of the other world.

However, this didn't happen suddenly. Before my spiritual heart opened, there was a period when I received a lot of inspiration. This was primarily because I continually pursued higher knowledge. The principle "Ask and it will be given to you" (Matthew 7:7) also holds true for receiving spiritual inspiration. If you continuously seek higher awareness, a higher level of enlightenment, and a higher ability to judge things, an outside power responds.

The second reason I was able to receive inspiration was purity of soul. As long as you seek knowledge simply as a means to an end, you will not be able to pass beyond this first stage of wisdom. I imagine that many of you studied in order to be successful in life—to get into a better school, to get a better job, or to get a promotion. However, you will never pass through the gate of the first stage of wisdom as long as you regard study as a means to an end, because this sort of attitude casts a shadow on the purity of your soul.

What is valuable in the pursuit of academic study is the effort you make trying to reach infinite wisdom. Until you understand this, as long as you pursue knowledge only as a means of achieving some worldly end, you will not get beyond the first stage. Knowledge and learning should be your aim. When you come to a point where you regard learning as an end in itself, where you find joy in the pursuit of knowledge and feel your soul being refined through this pursuit, you have reached the goal of the first stage of wisdom.

This is also the first stage in the pursuit of enlightenment. Gradually you come to receive inspiration and experience moments of bliss, or extreme happiness, quite often. As you read hundreds of books, you may come across one or two that are very impressive, which touch you or move you to tears. Perhaps you will have the experience of listening to an inspiring talk and being so moved that you cannot stop cry-

---

*When we get rid of all the clouds that cover the mind, the spiritual heart opens and we become able to communicate directly with our guardians and guiding spirits.

ing. These experiences give you intense feelings of happiness, "the soul's joy."

It is as if a veil has been lifted and you are able to see the true state of the world. Before this, you may think people are trying to harm you or obstruct your path, or that things often do not go as you might wish, but once such negative ideas dissolve, you discover that the world is truly magnificent. Helen Keller wrote about this in her autobiography, *The Story of My Life* (New York: Doubleday, Page & Company, 1905). Despite her blindness, she experienced the world as a truly wonderful place.

The main character in *A Christmas Carol,* by Charles Dickens, illustrates a similar transformation. As you may recall, Scrooge is a crabby old fellow whose only concern is making money. Late one Christmas Eve, Scrooge meets three ghosts—the ghost of the past, the ghost of the present, and the ghost of the future. Each, in turn, shows Scrooge scenes from his life: The ghost of the past shows him how many people have suffered because of the way he has lived, caring only about making money. The ghost of the present shows him people he knows who are suffering even on Christmas Eve. Then the ghost of the future shows him how he will die, miserable and unloved.

After seeing these scenes, Scrooge begins to repent deeply. He reflects on himself and realizes what a false life he's been living, how many people he has hurt, and how ignorant he has been of other people's pain. As dawn breaks, a completely different world unfolds before his eyes, and he has a truly wonderful Christmas. Everyone seems remarkable, and Scrooge's bitter expression had been replaced by a bright smile, which is greeted with smiles. He realizes that the same world he used to see as ugly now looks beautiful. His world is transformed simply by the change in his state of mind.

Dickens created this story with exquisite skill, revealing his own enlightenment. Like Dickens, those who have passed through the first stage of wisdom see this world as a truly wonderful place.

At this stage, enlightenment is still rather fragile. In an isolated and tranquil environment where there is no cause for concern, you can probably maintain your peace of mind and remain free of worldly cares, but there is still the possibility this state can be shaken. It corresponds to the Arhat level in the stages of enlightenment, the upper level of the sixth dimension, where the soul is still vulnerable to "rust" and falling from grace.

To put it another way, at the moment of "conversion,"* the turning point from a secular to a religious life, everyone can experience a fresh, new state. Unfortunately, this feeling of renewal doesn't last long in humdrum, daily living. To advance to the second stage of wisdom, you need to discover how to overcome this fragility, how to maintain this sense of freshness and continue to experience a completely changed view of the world.

At the first stage of wisdom, your level of awareness is quite high, so it's easy to find fault with others. You will be able to clearly see others' problems, worries, and weaknesses, but this isn't enough. You need to embrace people, despite their shortcomings, with a love born of an even higher perspective. If you lose yourself in daily life or are lacking in love for others, your uneven pursuit of wisdom will reveal that you have not yet established an unshakable state of mind.

Establishing Unshakable Confidence in Your Wisdom

One requirement for achieving the second stage of wisdom is steady diligence in study and learning. You need to make a constant, sincere effort to accumulate knowledge, and not put any kind of limits on this effort.

You must be like conifers, evergreens that never lose their green color, even in winter. In autumn, the leaves of many trees turn red or yellow before falling to the ground, but pines and cedars remain green. We know from experience that although they blend in with the other

---

*"Conversion" here means the realization that you have been living mistakenly, your mind is unrighteous, and you are being swayed by worldly desires, which causes you to turn your mind to the world of faith.

trees in summer, they are in stark contrast to white snow. It is important that you stand your ground like these conifers, even if your circumstances change. Your challenge is to sustain the effort you make with the passing of time. If you have an important exam or anticipate promotion, you usually have the motivation to work hard. When these "carrots," or opportunities to succeed, are dangled before you, you can gallop like a horse, but can you sustain that motivation if the carrot is taken away? The longer you can maintain your enthusiasm, the higher your spiritual status.

What impresses me most about the lives of great historical figures is their strong resolve and spirit of perseverance.[4] No matter what difficulties they faced, no matter what suffering they endured, they never gave up; they always made an effort to overcome every hardship. Through this sustained effort, their inner glow became more brilliant. Experiencing hardship is essential for strengthening the soul.

If you want to see someone's true nature, you need only observe that person on two occasions—at a high point of success and in the depths of disappointment. Those who become conceited following small successes do not achieve great success; they are quickly satisfied, and as soon as they begin to attract the attention of others and are regarded as important, they begin to boast.

On the other hand, those who succumb to despair when faced with failure, who only complain and grumble, do not achieve success either. The length of time you are able to tolerate hardship while continuing to refine and strengthen yourself is the test of your true stature.

When your status suddenly improves, how do you react? If you soon grow proud, you cannot be regarded as a person of true stature. The higher your position, the more you need to continue making an effort and the more humble you need to become. If you maintain this attitude, you will surely achieve great success.

The second stage of wisdom is a period of endurance, and of steadily building self-confidence. The key to building confidence in yourself is to have experiences of success, and to broaden your perspective in different ways. If you fail to build an unshakable confidence in your own wisdom while you are in the stage of establishing yourself, you eventually will become jealous of others. You'll feel insecure and envious when you see someone at the same stage who seems more competent than you, or who achieves something remarkable. If you feel jealous, it means you've not yet reached the second stage.

If you are constantly and steadfastly absorbed in improving yourself, your mind won't be swayed by the successes or failures of others. There are those who feel happy when others fail, or who suffer pangs of jealousy when others succeed. These people have not yet established an unshakable confidence in their own wisdom, or confidence in their own enlightenment and awareness. They have not yet firmly established a right way of seeing others, the world, and themselves. This stage tests your goals and your diligence, and can last a long time. Many can't get beyond it in one lifetime, but once you do, you are able to give unconditional love to others. If you build strong confidence in your own wisdom, you are free of jealousy and emanate a gentle light. The first stage of wisdom is a period of strenuous self-discipline, so the light you emit may be too glaring. But when you reach the second stage, you take a step forward and are able to extend great love to others.

The Wisdom to Serve Others

People do not usually get beyond the second stage of wisdom, but there are higher levels where wisdom takes flight beyond the sphere of the individual mind. In the first and second stages, the development of wisdom is confined to the individual. A person's wisdom is simply the knowledge and skill to solve personal, everyday problems and engender peace of mind and a sense of happiness. At the third stage, however, wisdom reaches beyond individual boundaries to become something higher. This level of wisdom is not simply a collection of information or skills, but knowledge that is transformed into love. As knowledge is transformed into love, it becomes established as a fine philosophy to be shared with many.

Thinkers who present original ideas to the world through their writings or lectures are often at the third stage of wisdom. Unless an author has attained the third stage of wisdom, a book can neither truly move people nor last to influence future generations. At this stage, both the quality and quantity of a thinker's awareness are transformed into great wisdom, becoming a treasure for all humanity. Wisdom extends beyond the individual and is shared with many, inspiring and encouraging the spiritual evolution of souls.

This transformation requires many spiritual experiences, either through an encounter with someone who has had these sorts of experiences or through a major shift in your perception of life. Just leading an ordinary life will not take someone to this third stage. Just before attaining this stage, people become convinced that the thoughts they have contemplated over and over can be of benefit to others and serve to guide them. This is the stage when learning is transformed into a love that serves others. It corresponds to advancing from the Light Realm of the sixth dimension to the Bodhisattva Realm of the seventh dimension in the spirit world. It is a shift from the world of intellectual pursuit to the world of love. Only when you explore knowledge with the strong desire to be of service to many, and actually translate this into action, have you reached the Bodhisattva level.

What is needed most today is this level of true wisdom, a wisdom that embraces love. Unfortunately, many individuals appear content to remain on a merely intellectual and individualistic level. However, you should aim to reach the third stage of wisdom, the state of Bodhisattva, where wisdom is an investment that can be harvested in the future. Aim to provide others with the fruits of your efforts, rather than enjoying them for yourself. Continually explore ways to translate and convey to others the wisdom that you have attained, to encourage them, inspire their souls, and illuminate their lives.

Fundamental Thought

There is, of course, an even higher stage of wisdom—the great wisdom of the Tathagata of the eighth and higher dimensions. In this stage of wisdom, a person not only knows the secrets of successful living, but also explores and discovers the treasures of humanity. In this fourth stage, wisdom becomes fundamental, like the wisdom of Socrates, Plato, and Aristotle in Greece; Confucius in China; Jesus in Palestine; or Shakyamuni Buddha in India.* These great figures introduced original thought that changed not only people, but also eras, cultures, and entire civilizations. Their great wisdom, attained through numerous incarnations and continuous effort, represents a source of wisdom beyond the wisdom of Bodhisattva, which embraces love. Great guiding spirits of light come to this world to teach the Truth, to create a new history for humanity, and to transform people, eras, and civilizations.

I continue to strive to firmly establish the Laws, condensing their wisdom and translating them into a universal love that transcends this age, so that they may be left for future generations. You also should take this opportunity to explore the development of wisdom.

---

*The spiritual Truth about these great figures of the past is described in *The Golden Laws*.

◀ PART THREE ▶

The Creation of an Ideal World

Now I would like to present the principles of utopia, salvation, self-reflection, and prayer. The principle of self-reflection is particularly powerful; it is a kind of sequel to the principle of enlightenment. This section is highly recommended for anyone troubled by negative spiritual influences, because this principle is endowed with the spiritual power of Buddha that can repel any evil spirits, no matter how strong. The principle of utopia guides the establishment of utopia in both the outer world and the inner world. The dawn of a new age of humanity is near.

SEVEN

The Principle of Utopia

The Guiding Principles for Establishing Utopia in Our Inner and Outer Worlds

Humankind is in a period of transition; there will be many difficulties to overcome, and we must prepare steadfastly in order to usher in a new utopian age. There are several guiding elements that constitute the principle of utopia.

Establishing the Age of Spirituality

We must first inaugurate the age of spirituality. If we do not institute a spiritual age now, we will lose the chance forever. If crises occur, we cannot simply dismiss them as crises, nor should we be content to escape them. We must realize that these crises are all part of a drama being directed by God. We live in difficult times at a turning point in history, but we can take advantage of this reality to make great strides and move in the direction of establishing a spiritual age. It is important to use every opportunity to move forward in the direction of development, and to lay foundations for the future.

In Japan, it is said that only about 20 percent of the population believes in the existence of the spirit world, or that the soul is the essential core of our being. Why is it that people in these evolved times do not accept the absolute and ultimate Truth, which has existed for hundreds of millions of years? How is it possible to live each day without knowing the Truth? What kind of people are we? What is the basis for contemporary existence? As we ask ourselves these questions, we cannot possibly deny that our present-day civilization is built totally on delusions.

I have passed on messages from high spirits in heaven, who work in many different ways to provide proof of the existence of the Real World. What they really want to tell us is simple: Whether or not people on earth are able to see or accept it, the other world truly does exist. Just as there are countries such as Japan and the United States, there really is a spirit world.

The law of reincarnation, too, is easily understood in the Real World, where we return after we leave this world. In the Real World, reincarnation is as simple as first-grade arithmetic. Yet this simple fact is incomprehensible to many of the so-called intellectual elite of the present age. What sort of knowledge have such intellectuals accumulated? What do they think they are learning? In reality, it amounts to nothing more than a collection of unnecessary information.

Now is the time to reexamine all that we believe in, all that we value. We are living at the climax of God's dramatic scenario. Our mission in this era is far greater than we imagine: The breadth and depth of the Truth, and the number of people to whom we must convey it, is vast and overwhelming. However, the Truth must filter into every corner of the world as quickly as possible, and I continuously search for the most efficient method to achieve this goal.

The Reformation of Economic Principles

In order to launch a new era, it is first necessary to establish the age of spirituality. The next requirement is a reformation of economic principles. Over the last few hundred years, the economic system that has prevailed throughout the world and is now taken for granted is capitalism. However, is capitalism really the best system?

To put it bluntly, the present system is misguided. The majority of people who work for a living believe the pursuit of profit to be the ideal—the highest principle. Seeking financial gain or profit isn't wrong, but people must be clear about their reason for pursuing it. If you own or work for a company, you probably know how important it is to make a profit. Why is it so necessary? This philosophy of chasing profit alone is a contemporary form of "misguided religion." The human soul has been poisoned by this kind of belief.

The profits of economic activity are acceptable only when they are used for a positive purpose, whether passive or active. Not pursuing profits that might corrupt others is a passive purpose, whereas an active purpose pursues profit to bring happiness to others. The worship of profit becomes evil when these two conditions are ignored.

Today profit has become a kind of false god that results in the idolatry of numbers. This perverted worship of materialism, this present-day worship of Baal, is raging and must be rooted out. In an economic system, profit should serve the true needs of humanity. People are employed in a variety of activities, and our monetary value system is one of the standards by which we evaluate those activities. This method of evaluation, however, is still primitive.

In the Real World, there is also an economic system based on money. For example, in the Posthumous Realm of the fourth dimension, a currency is in use because the inhabitants there feel the need of it. Of course, the currency is not made of matter; it is created in the world of thought. In the fifth dimensional world, there is an economy based on a sort of exchange system. This notion operates up to the Light Realm of the sixth dimension. There, values are no longer measured in money, but by the amount of gratitude a person receives—a spiritual currency.

In the worlds above that, the economic system is one of divine light. The amount of light given by God is the manifestation of the value of people's behavior and actions. One way this is measured is by an aura, or halo, which represents God's currency. Those who have achieved a considerable amount will receive an equivalent amount of recognition, or light, which accumulates to create a halo. In the sense that it can be accumulated, light operates in the same way that money functions on earth. Light is given according to the quality and amount of good work that is accomplished in accordance with God's will. This is the economics that operates in the world of Truth.

However, this does not occur only in the higher world. To a certain extent, the same system also operates in this earthly world. Perhaps you cannot see the amount of light you receive from God, but the effects manifest in various forms, such as good health and success. At other times, this God-given currency may manifest as good character. So, the operative economy of the kingdom of God is also relevant in this world.

There are two kinds of currency in circulation on earth. One is government currency; the other is the currency issued by God. These are not always completely separate, and in some instances can be interchangeable; in certain markets both are valid. Our target is to establish a new economic system where these two currencies blend and the tides meet. The economy must move in the direction of the confluence of worldly values and the values of Truth, reflecting the will of God, creating economic principles that are valid in both worlds.

Two thousand years ago, Jesus talked of realizing the kingdom of God within, saying "Give to Caesar what is Caesar's, and to God what is God's" (Mark 12:17) and "Repent, for the kingdom of heaven is near" (Matthew 3:2). While the kingdom of God of which Jesus spoke did not extend beyond the inner world, the kingdom of God we are now trying to establish encompasses both the inner and the outer worlds. Our mission in this lifetime will not be accomplished unless this earthly world is transformed into a heaven.

The Research and Establishment of Principles for Action

If our aim were to focus solely on the kingdom of the mind, there would be no reason for us to begin missionary work in this present age, or for me to dedicate myself wholeheartedly to giving lectures to whomever will listen. That has been done for two thousand, three thousand, ten thousand, even a hundred thousand years. We cannot repeat the same effort each time we reincarnate; we must move forward to achieve higher goals.

To this end, the principles behind our actions can be reduced to two categories. One principle is the repentance of the individual—the principle of personal enlightenment; the other is the repentance of society as a whole, the principle governing the reformation of society. Without these principles, it is not possible to effect change in this age. They are like two swords, one short, the other long. With these two swords we can bring about a global reformation.

So the third pillar that is essential in creating the kingdom of God is researching and establishing two major principles for action that will reform both the individual and society as a whole.

The First Principle for Action to Create an Ideal World—Utopia in the Mind

The first stage in creating an ideal world is to govern the kingdom within. To this end, I have introduced the four principles of happiness: love, wisdom, self-reflection, and progress. This teaching is a modern interpretation of Buddhism, which focuses on the individual search for enlightenment.

Creating utopia begins with the principle of the mind, and teachings about the mind. Why do you incarnate in many different eras, playing many different roles? Had you wanted to be a king, you could have incarnated as a king in every lifetime, but in the course of many different incarnations, no one chooses to be royalty every time. People take different roles as they follow the path of enlightenment. Sometimes they are born kings, sometimes beggars, sometimes middle-class citizens, and so on.

There is a basic law, an important guiding principle running through the entire universe, that states, "Regardless of your environment, govern the kingdom within and establish utopia in your own mind." This unspoken law has remained unchanged throughout the long history of humankind.

How can you create an ideal world in your own mind right now? What do you need to do to bring the kingdom of God that Jesus taught closer? You must at least know about the lives and thoughts of those people who succeeded in governing the kingdom of God within.

In order to show the kinds of thoughts that are necessary to be able to govern the kingdom of God within, I publish many books on the Truth. In my books, I give examples of the kinds of thoughts and actions that lead to heaven. Look at the way you think and live in the light of the Truth. If you feel that your thought patterns accord with the Truth, you are fortunate and can continue living as you do now.

Unfortunately, many people have not yet reached this level. Imagine if you were to die at this very moment and become a spiritual being: what lessons have you learned in this life that you could pass on? Would you be able to say anything important, anything of value? In my books, I present ideal ways of living as models for you to follow.

The Determination to Reform the Self

After studying examples you can follow, the next challenge is to find your own way. First, turn your vision inward and ask if you have the will to transform yourself. This is the starting point, as well as the pre-requisite for joining Happy Science. The exploration of Right Mind is crucial in our fellowship. Many people believe themselves to be doing well, but have only a superficial understanding. Are you really willing to transform your mind?

Very few people today live in complete harmony with God's will. In fact, the majority of people do not. Since this is the case, the exploration of Right Mind naturally requires self-transformation. Are you willing to correct the way you think and behave, and make changes as soon as you see mistakes? If you are satisfied with yourself as you are now, and cannot see any need to change or improve, then you haven't even reached the starting point.

The exploration of Right Mind is by no means just an abstract idea; it implies the willingness to change, and to invest energy in self-transformation. Are you willing to change your attitudes? If not, you are welcome to part company with Happy Science; our teachings are not for those who have no intention of improving themselves. If you are studying the Truth and find that you have not yet established the kingdom of God in your own mind, you will need to correct your thoughts and change yourself. If you think that you have already attained the highest wisdom, you are welcome to start your own movement or to continue to live in a completely separate world. This may sound harsh, but those who are satisfied with the way they are and don't have the will to transform themselves do not deserve to be called seekers of Truth.

There is a great gap between the state of mind of those who live in our three-dimensional world and that of the inhabitants of the Real World of the fourth dimension and beyond. From the perspective of high spirits in the Real World, this world appears uncertain and unstable. Living here is like walking on the bottom of the sea, or through a mirage in a desert. That uncertainty is why you must not be content to remain as you are now.

Unless you have the strong determination to change yourself, change will not happen. Straighten out your mind and start anew. Motivate yourself; be determined to establish the kingdom of God within. This is the starting point, which in Buddhism is called "bodhi-mind," or *bodhicitta,* in Sanskrit.* Shakyamuni Buddha emphasized the importance of this aspiration to achieve enlightenment. People cannot change unless they aspire to change. Do people change if they receive a large sum of money? Perhaps they are different for a while, but deep down they do not change. How about if they are given a house? They may change for a while, but their basic nature remains unchanged. There is no other way to establish the kingdom within except to transform your own mind. No one else can do this for you.

The kingdom is within each one of you, and each one of you has been given the key to open it. There is no duplicate key. Unless you

---

*Bodhi-mind, or bodhicitta, means an aspiration for enlightenment, or a will or desire to achieve enlightenment.

open it with the key you carry within you, the door to the kingdom of your mind cannot be opened. Having been given all these tools, now you must awaken to this simple truth: a very strong determination will give you the strength of will to transform yourself.

There is a gap between your present state of being and the state God wishes for you. I feel the burning passion of the high spirits; they are eager to awaken people on earth, and they earnestly wish people to know the Truth. But no matter how passionately, how fervently they try to communicate their messages, people on earth disregard these messages as merely words in books. They don't realize that high spirits have put their hearts and souls into their messages.

Imagine that you have left this world to become an angel in the other world. How would you feel observing the present state of people on this earth? What would you do? I am deeply aware of how intently the high spirits are watching over and trying to guide us, but regrettably, I cannot convey fully what I perceive.

Nevertheless, I can say at least that you have the key. Take the key in your hand, the key that is within you. Put it into the keyhole and open the door of your mind. Unless each person truly awakens to the kingdom of God within, the energy for salvation will not pour forth.

Sometimes you may feel that God is unjust. You may ask yourself why there are such vast differences in people's living conditions, environments, gifts and abilities, houses, parents, family backgrounds, incomes, physical strength, and so on. You may blame God and think him unjust to allow these differences to exist, but in one respect God treats us all equally: God has given each one of us the key to open the inner door. We are absolutely equal in this respect.

Building an Inner Store and Taking Action

First you need a strong will and the energy to achieve self-transformation. After the strength of will has been awakened, there are two steps necessary for the next stage.

The first step is to build an inner store of spiritual nourishment.

Before we are born on earth, God gives each of us a certain amount of spiritual "funds" for travel expenses during our journey from birth to death. However, people use this up on trifles along the way, forgetting the main purpose of their journey. Instead of using this precious gift for its intended purpose, they often squander it on unimportant things. Stop doing this; otherwise, you won't be able to reach your destination. Look back to your starting point and start accumulating the energy of light, the knowledge of Truth, and the energy of love. It is important to start saving your travel expenses again, because they're almost gone. This is one of the next steps you need to take after determining to transform yourself.

For more than forty years, Shakyamuni Buddha repeatedly taught the importance of inner accumulation, of building a store of inner spiritual nourishment. The nourishment stored in one's mind serves to enrich the minds of others. This storehouse becomes the source from which you are able to give to countless others.

There are many types of offerings, but the offering of Dharma, of teaching the Law, is by far the greatest. Unless you have an inner store of the Truth, it is impossible to practice the offering of Dharma. This is why I speak repeatedly of the importance of learning the Truth. This is the order that must be followed: Explore the Truth, study it, and then convey it to others.

Let me explain each element of this sequence, one at a time. Exploring the Truth means taking an interest in the Truth, accumulating knowledge and information with a specific purpose in mind, and constantly storing knowledge of the Truth for the future.

Studying the Truth means assimilating the knowledge that you have accumulated and making it your own, honing it so that you will be able to fight with it as a weapon when necessary. It is not enough just to collect many different teachings of the Truth randomly; you need to be ready to make active use of them. Don't be satisfied just to read books of Truth. Think about how you can make their wisdom your own, and use the information for the next step of your development.

Establish your own methods of applying the teachings to your life.

Unquestioning acceptance of what is written, and simple remembrance of what you have read or heard, is not "study." Your study must go deeper. Ask yourself how you can apply the Truth to your everyday life, to yourself and your circumstances. From this perspective, reintegrate and reorganize the Truth within you. Only when you do this can you say that you are studying the Truth.

There are two aspects to the second stage of creating utopia in the mind. After inner accumulation comes the practice of taking action and conveying the Truth to others. After you have truly studied your accumulated knowledge, how are you going to present it to others? The deeper your study, the more able you are to teach others. The wider your knowledge, the more active you will be in different ways.

The poverty of contemporary religion lies in its inability to present its teachings in ways that are appropriate to the circumstances and state of mind of those who receive them. This is why many religious organizations are now regarded as cults, and best avoided. These religions believe that only their own teachings are right; as soon as they receive spiritual messages, they try to force them onto others, without first examining them. This is the wrong attitude when it comes to conveying the Truth to others. You must first collect the materials for knowledge, then incorporate them into your own life and thoughts. Once you have done so, then speak about the Truth in your own words. It is important to absorb the Truth until it is incorporated into your every action.

If you are learning from lectures and books of the Truth, study them deeply until you even forget that you have ever studied them, until you feel they were originally part of you. Only then can you talk to others about the different teachings in your own words, expressing the Truth through your actions in a natural yet unique way. It is no use pointing out to someone a specific part of a book you have read. If, in a book of the Truth, you find something that resonates deep in your heart, something that touches your soul, make it your own. Transform it into your own philosophy, your own personal creed.

Once you have made a creed your own, begin to take action as a small part of the kingdom of God. I emphasize the process of studying the Truth before conveying it to others, because it is here that mistakes and confusion arise in religious circles.

Problems occur when people try to convert others before they have assimilated what they have learned. They have not managed to govern their own kingdom within, yet they go to their neighbors and, with their own key, try to open the lock of their neighbors' minds. It is the responsibility of each and every person to open the lock of his or her own mind. If you want to encourage others to unlock their minds, you must have had the experience of opening your own mind with your own key.

First of all, you must perceive the kingdom of God for yourself, to feel and be sure of the way God wishes you to live. Then you will experience peace of mind and great joy, and a sense of being reborn. If you have not experienced this feeling welling up from within, the feeling of being born anew and becoming a different person, it means that your mind has not yet been unlocked. So probe deep into your inner self until you truly feel you have been reborn.

Those who are elated by a shallow sense of satisfaction create confusion. It is my wish for more and more people to part company with the shallow, false self, and experience the overwhelming joy of discovering the true self, the self that God has always loved. I sincerely hope that you will experience moments of deep, incomparable bliss in this lifetime. I want to help you savor this bliss, and to know how magnificent true happiness feels.

One of my most important missions is to help people experience this joy. If they can experience it while they are alive, there will be no confusion in the next life, no suffering in the other world.

People carry their unresolved problems over to the other world and continue to suffer there. But worries and problems must be solved in this lifetime. The liberation or emancipation* that Buddhism teaches doesn't necessarily mean returning to higher spiritual realms, never being born in this world again. What liberation truly means is casting

---

*Liberation, or emancipation, is a state of mind in which you are free from worldly attachment and limitations.

off the heavy armor of three-dimensional concerns. Take off your armor to reveal the diamond self.* Everyone has a heavy suit of iron armor covering the heart and mind—you walk around rattling. Be aware of how ridiculous this looks from a spiritual perspective.

In the eyes of high spirits, everyone on earth is rattling. If you were one of these high spirits, you would surely want to do something to lighten people's loads. First, take off your own armor. Experience the lightness you feel and how pleasant that feeling is. To experience this, you must first generate the energy for self-transformation, then make a serious study of the Truth, then master it.

Finally, you must put it into practice in everyday life. Once you truly understand how much grace you receive from God, this knowledge will lead to action. Any knowledge that is not converted into action is not true knowledge. When you truly know, when you have truly studied, your body will move of its own accord; your feet, hands, and mouth will be restless to convey the Truth. Once you experience this stage, knowledge is no longer simply parroting someone else's words—it is authentic.

Knowing the True Nature of the Spirit World

The third requirement for establishing utopia in the mind is to acquire the knowledge of a world that you did not know existed. You must see and experience the true nature of the spirit world, of the Bodhisattva Realm of the seventh dimension and the Tathagata Realm of the eighth dimension.

It is important to come to know these realms while you are still living in the physical world. We were not born into this lifetime on earth merely to return to the same realm of heaven from which we came. Rather, the aim of this lifetime is to become an angel of light through undergoing different experiences. When the world faces hardships, more light is needed, and more people are required to act as angels of light. If the supply of angels of light sent from the Real World is not sufficient,

---

*The diamond self is the true nature of a human being, a child of God. The diamond self is the Buddha-nature, the divine nature that shines like a diamond.

countless angels of light must be produced through life on earth. Before the creation of angels of light, "warriors of light"* must also come forward, people able to fight on God's behalf.

We cannot wait for great souls to reincarnate from the other world and start teaching the Law. Unless people of great potential emerge from among those now living, the movement for salvation will not be launched. Don't wait for high spirits to be sent from heaven; become a representative of the great spirit yourself. Become a Bodhisattva, an angel of light, in this lifetime. Become a Tathagata, a great angel of light, while you are on this earth. What is the purpose of this life, if not to attain these high states?

If you have completed a thorough study of the Truth, mastered the Truth, and put it into practice, you will be able to attain the state of Bodhisattva, or even of Tathagata. You have the materials, so it is up to you to make the effort. I would like you to discover the Truth and become a Bodhisattva, an angel of light. I hope for the emergence of one thousand Bodhisattvas on earth, for the emergence of some extraordinary Tathagatas from among you. Come forward, Bodhisattvas! Come forward, Tathagatas! The world needs light!

There's no need to concern yourself with past lives. A past life is a past life, and this life is this life. Make an effort to become an embodiment of light in this life. Don't concern yourself with how long it may take others to accomplish this—it could be several hundred, several thousand, or tens of thousands of years. In the world of Truth, there is no such thing as average speed. The moment you think wisely, you are transformed. This is the nature of the world of Truth. In the world of the mind, in the world of the soul, time does not really exist, so the very moment you think a thought, things change. This is the state that Zen Buddhists have ultimately tried to achieve.†

---

*Warriors of light are those who continue their spiritual discipline with the aim of becoming angels of light. They have awakened to spiritual Truth and, aware of their mission, are working actively to create utopia on earth.
†Zen Buddhism was founded in China by Bodhidharma (446–528 CE). Followers try to attain enlightenment by means of practicing *zazen* (sitting meditation).

Become a Bodhisattva or a Tathagata in this very moment! You already have all you need, so why not take up the challenge? Why not take action, make a move while there is an earth where you can work and over six billion people for the sake of whom you can act? All these people are waiting for you to take action, so what are you waiting for? There is no time to waste. Stand up and make a move.

Make sure you have a firm grasp of the three steps for building utopia within, but then do not hesitate to become a Bodhisattva or a Tathagata. If you feel you're not quite ready for these levels, then at least have the fortitude to become a warrior of light, and fight to establish the kingdom of God on earth. Out of this effort, new angels of light will be born. With effort, anyone can reach the level of a warrior of light. That should be your goal in life.

Many spiritual messages have come to me from heaven, and I've published these in books, but for what purpose? Why do so many high spirits send me messages? Why does Jesus send me spiritual messages? Why does Moses?

What is happening now before your very eyes is something that happens only once every few thousand years—the creation of a Golden Age. You are reading and studying the Truth, so you should work to create a Golden Age for the future. If you don't create this Golden Age, who will? The people of the future? The people of the past? Who, exactly? The principle of utopia at the level of the individual means nothing less than becoming an angel of light. If more and more people become angels of light, this earth will be transformed into a Buddha land, an ideal world. The greater the number of angels of light who come forward, the greater their power to create an ideal world.

The Second Principle for Action to Create an Ideal World—Utopia in Society

For the next step to an ideal world we must create utopia in society. We must allow the Truth—the "written proof" given by God—to manifest in this three-dimensional world as "theoretical proof" and "actual proof."*

Who will prove the authenticity of what is written? Those who have read and understood the Truth. They will prove it by using the laws of the mind to change society. You may read and understand, for example, that new economic principles based on the Truth need to be established, but you also can demonstrate what can happen in society when these principles are put into practice. Nothing changes unless you put the Truth into practice where you live and work.

It is important to think about how to apply the Truth in this three-dimensional world, how to clarify the logic of Truth according to the law of cause and effect, and how to explain it scientifically as theoretical proof. We must prove that society can be reformed, and that by acting in accordance with God's will, we can transform this earth into a Buddha land. Unless we prove it in this three-dimensional world, and confirm it with our own eyes, we haven't truly accomplished anything.

Don't be satisfied with subjective opinions and judgments. Don't become elated by personal satisfaction or intoxicated by your own well-being. Experience for yourself that changes really do occur, that society can be reformed, that the world can change, and that people's minds can change. You must prove that this actually does happen.

Furthermore, the transformation that occurs within individuals must become a great tide of love with the power to influence and transform the minds of many. We must prove that what is truly of value in this world cannot be seen. What is not visible to the eye—God, love, compassion, courage, and faith—has true value, and is meaningful and significant. We are living in a great river of love, a world full of invisible worth. The principle of utopia will truly manifest only when everyone knows and experiences this reality. In this society, where people only believe in what they can see, let us launch a movement to show people the inestimable value of what is not visible.

---

*"Written proof" refers to the well-structured teachings left behind in the form of writing. "Theoretical proof" refers to theories that are logically consistent and rational. "Actual proof" means the actual occurrence of miracles or phenomena that are beyond human understanding. Authentic Truth is supported by all three types of proof.

EIGHT

The Principle of Salvation

Make Innovations and New Discoveries

Those who have just begun to study the Truth should be aware that the way your life unfolds, and the way you transform yourself through encountering the Truth, depends on the discoveries you make in your everyday life. While it is easy to say that making discoveries is important, very few people actually remember this in day-to-day living. How you get closer to the core of the Truth and live in harmony with God's will depends on the effort you make each day to discover new things. This accumulation of discoveries gives the soul depth.

Life flows along quite monotonously for those who live each day without discovering something new, but for those who endeavor to glean new wisdom every day, life is immensely exciting. If you make discovering something new each day your personal, continual challenge, that alone enables you to say that your day has been worth living. I don't ask this only of you; every day I do my utmost to discover something new and bring ingenuity to my work. In July of 1988, I published five new books in a month. People wonder how I could possibly have published so many books in such a short period. The answer lies in my constant endeavor to devise new ways of doing things.

It would be impossible to write so many manuscripts by hand. Some writers dictate their work, but you could produce only one book a month that way. When I produce a book, I plan the layout of the chapters and sections beforehand, then I give lectures based on these outlines. When a lecture is over and the transcript has been typeset, I have the complete manuscript of a book in my hand.

Usually, the transcribed draft of a lecture needs to be edited, and paragraphs deleted and added, but since each lecture is based on an outline, my books are created much more quickly. This cannot happen solely through relying on spiritual guidance; it requires personal effort and ingenuity. You, too, can accomplish a great deal if you devise new ways of doing things.

In order to launch a movement for human salvation, you can't just run around with a slogan. In a sense, the logic of business also operates in the world of Truth. The world of business demands a constant increase in quality and quantity; there is always a struggle between this demand and human limitations. The only way to solve that struggle is to find new ways to accomplish things. When conveying the Truth to the world, it is also essential to use innovation and devise new approaches.

To launch a movement for true salvation, we need more ingenuity and discovery. The typical approach to missionary work is inadequate. Each person lives in a different environment, is engaged in different work, holds a different position, and has a different amount of free time.

Under such circumstances, how will you convey the Truth? It is the nature of Truth to transmit itself and spread, so how are you going to allow it to spread in your life? This is a difficult challenge. However, if you put your mind to it, you can certainly discover hundreds of ingenious ways to convey the Truth to others.

The path of missionary work will vary according to your occupation, your gender, and your environment. If you work in a downtown office, for example, you can find fitting ways to study the Truth and spread this knowledge in business circles. If you live in the countryside, there must be a unique way to spread this message. If you work in the home, you can find your own way to function as a powerful force for conveying the Truth. Make repeated efforts to discover new and original ways to spread knowledge within the context of your unique occupation, position, and environment.

In exploring Right Mind, you will learn how to control your mind so that you are blessed with a richer and happier life. However, I am speaking generally, and what I say may not always correspond to your particular situation. So you must use ingenuity to find ways of using and applying these teachings in order to solve your own problems. Occasionally I offer question-and-answer sessions about people's suffering, and on reading some of these, you may find situations similar to your own.[1] No two problems are exactly alike, but you may discover how to control and manage your own mind using ideas from these examples.

Learning is not limited to an intellectual understanding of lectures or seminars. Learning how to apply each teaching to your own personal problems is demanding work. Only after you have tackled your problems and overcome your suffering or unhappiness will you have any powers of persuasion or reach a level where you can speak confidently about what you've learned. Then, when you talk to other people, you may find that their situations are quite different. Can the lessons you've learned through your own experiences apply directly to others?

This is another difficult challenge, and it is here that problems often occur in connection with religious organizations. People who belong to certain religions tend to think their experiences are best, and, believing they are recommending a panacea, try to force others to think or do as they do. This can result in disappointment or avoidance.

You must find a way to overcome this barrier. The first stage is to be able to understand the other person. You need to know the person's background and experiences, what the person thinks and expects. As long as you are focused on only your own problems, your learning is limited to the issues that apply to your own specific circumstances.

However, as you progress to the stage where you start applying the lessons from your life to the circumstances of others, you will begin to find ingenious ways of bringing happiness not only into your own life, but also into the lives of others. This will, of course, result in other people's happiness, but over and above that, you will personally experience even greater happiness. It is similar to the effect of reading a novel; it allows you to experience a life that you never actually live.

When we are born into this world, each of us chooses the environment most appropriate for the development of our soul. Although your environment is the most fitting for you, it cannot offer you every possible experience. Even if you were to change jobs frequently throughout your lifetime, you could have twenty or thirty different jobs at most. It isn't possible to simultaneously be both a man and a woman, or to experience hundreds of different diseases within a single lifetime. As for losing a job, different patterns of unemployment exist in different types of businesses, and the lessons learned in each situation are different.

When someone is suffering due to life experiences quite different from yours, you will need to find new ways to apply the Truth more effectively. In this endeavor, you will gain nourishment for your own soul and learn valuable lessons. If you use your ingenuity to guide someone who is completely different from you, both lives will be enriched.

Making Your Life Richer and More Effective

No matter how complicated your chosen environment, the number of lessons you can learn in one lifetime is limited. People reincarnate into this world again and again. The ordinary person is reborn approximately once every three hundred years. The higher-level Bodhisattva souls from the seventh dimension reincarnate every eight hundred to a thousand years. The cycle of reincarnation for souls of the Tathagata level of the eighth dimension is once every one- or two thousand years.

To be born on this earth is a rare event, and the number of lessons you master in a single lifetime determines whether your life has been successful. With this in mind, consider how to increase the effectiveness and richness of your life. Rather than being satisfied just solving your own life problems, why not study the workbook of problems assigned to other people as well? It will expand your knowledge and give you the strength to solve a wide range of issues. Your effort will result in an accumulation of great inner wisdom, Prajna-Paramita,*² as nourishment for the soul. It is therefore necessary to be selfish in the truest sense. Being selfish in this context doesn't mean asserting yourself at the cost of others; rather, it means making the most of your few decades of life and harvesting the greatest possible crop from a single acre of time. Doing this is by no means going against God's will.

As you apply the Truth in a practical way to many different cases, you accumulate the experience to translate the Truth in a way that others can understand, and to utter words that will lend others strength to help them recover from life crises. There is boundless potential for this effort, and it is here that a path opens to the infinite evolution of your soul. The study of the Truth has no ceiling. As long as you study the Truth only at an intellectual level, there is a ceiling, but once you reach the stage of applying this knowledge in a practical way, all limits disappear and your learning will take an infinite variety of forms. This is the essence of the Law.

The Law is not fixed, but ever changing. It streams freely and selflessly, flowing like the water of a great river. It evaporates, turns into clouds and then into rain, and becomes a river once again. Like the river, the Law nourishes and enriches people's hearts and minds, changing into many different forms. The Law has no fixed characteristics or form of its own. Although it may take a certain form at a particular time, it warms the hearts of people in many different guises, in the everchanging process of transmutation.

---

*Prajna-Paramita (Sanskrit) is the perfection of wisdom. *Prajna* means "deep wisdom," or "transcendental wisdom," which wells up from within like an inexhaustible spring.

The Meaning of Transmigration
between Planets

The Law assumes different forms to guide people. As I mentioned in my other books, in the great universe there are actually a multitude of beings. Some belong to civilizations that are more advanced than ours, whereas other civilizations are more primitive. A civilization appropriate to the environment and the types of souls that reincarnate there evolve on each planet, and the Law assumes different forms for each planet.

There are many planets in this universe, each with a different pace of life, and each has its own spiritual discipline appropriate to its inhabitants. Our planet moves around the sun creating a year that consists of 365 days, and as it rotates on its axis, it creates a day of twenty-four hours. Imagine if there were a planet that revolved around the sun in just fifty days. If there were four seasons a year and a year was fifty days, a season would last for only about ten days. Once summer ended after ten days, in just a few days it would be autumn. Very soon, the leaves would have fallen and snow would arrive. Then just ten days later, spring would come. If people had such a short year, the cycle of their lives would be very swift, and the pace of life would be extremely fast.

There are two different types of people on earth: those who work at a hectic pace and those who live in a leisurely way. Some people are extremely busy working and accomplishing a great deal, thereby accumulating a wide variety of experiences in a single lifetime. When the souls of these people have very little left to learn on earth, they will likely reincarnate on a planet where the cycles are extremely rapid.

But even if these people can work exceptionally fast on earth and accomplish four or five times as much as others, when they go to a planet where a year lasts only fifty days, they will seem lethargic. The rhythm of life and the pace of work on earth will seem like a video in slow motion. Others on that planet will work much more quickly and their thoughts will be much faster. In order to keep up with them, the newcomers from earth will have to make a great deal of effort, thus progressing to the next stage of their spiritual development.

The opposite type of people appreciates the philosophy of stillness of Lao-tzu and Chuang-tzu,*³ and would rather stay home and meditate. They may think they lead the most peaceful life possible, but there is yet another planet where a year consists of a thousand days, allowing the inhabitants to be totally still and the pace of life to be even slower. On this planet, everything is very slow, even having a meal. When you sit at the table you contemplate the tableware for five or ten minutes, considering how it should be used, before taking your first mouthful. People who think of their way of life on earth as leisurely would be considered hectic. They would realize, "Even when I was meditating, I was bound by the concept of meditation. Unless I can live in a more relaxed way, free from all thought, my spiritual development will not be truly complete. I still have a long way to go before I achieve a state of oneness with nature."

There are also planets where the ratio of male to female inhabitants is unbalanced. For example, on a planet where only 10 percent of the population is female, women are extremely fertile and can give birth to five, six, or even ten children at a time. Like queen bees, they possess great authority, and are like goddesses in their realm. When these women become haughty and too accustomed to wielding power, they are sent to another planet where they are considered less important, and must start their spiritual development anew.

Although you may select an environment that is initially appropriate for your spiritual development, through the long process of repeated incarnations, the development of the soul becomes unbalanced by particular tendencies. Eventually, the time will come when it is too unbalanced to evolve in the expected direction. With each new epoch, there are still new opportunities for its development on earth,

---

*Lao-tzu (587–502 BCE) was the founder of Taoism. He taught that everyone should return to a life of ease and live at one with nature. Chuang-tzu (367–279 BCE) was his successor.

but the marginal utility* of the lessons of a soul is considerably diminished and the amount of nourishment that a soul can acquire in a single incarnation limited. When this happens, a human soul chooses to be born either in an environment that agrees completely with its own tendencies or in an environment that is completely different.

As you may have learned in my other books, Earth was formed about 4.6 billion years ago, when an asteroid was flung from its orbit around the sun. As this asteroid orbited independently, its mass increased. Gradually it cooled down until living creatures were able to live on its surface. This was, of course, a part of the Plan, forming different environments to create a range of life experiences. There have been several migrations from other planets to Earth, occurring at intervals of every few hundred million years since the Earth's formation. Many souls have come to Earth, which serves as a new training ground for these souls.

The Splitting of Souls

This is not to say that all human souls have migrated from other planets; there are also souls whose origin is on this planet. As a soul's energy level increases, it becomes difficult to remain one single individual. The amount of energy can become so vast that the soul splits into a number of spirits. Spirits of the ninth dimension are capable of splitting into tens of thousands, millions, or even hundreds of millions of entities. The amount of energy that can be contained within one physical body is limited, so spirits that embody vast amounts of energy must divide.

In the oldest books of Japanese history, *Kojiki* and *Nihon-Shoki,* there are many mythological tales recounting how different gods were born. For example, when a god was washing his ears in a river, another god was born from them; the same thing happened from his eyes and mouth. In these tales, both male and female were capable of giving

---

Marginal utility is a term used in economics to refer to the additional satisfaction or benefit to a consumer with the purchase of additional units of a commodity or service. As more units are purchased, the satisfaction gained will diminish.

birth. Although it sounds very mystical, this story actually illustrates in a symbolic way how energy can divide to create a number of spirits.

Spirits splinter into many entities to bring about the greatest expression of happiness. That one person can achieve happiness and develop greatness of character through attaining higher enlightenment is quite wonderful, but imagine the joy of thousands of people sharing that same experience. The joy would surely be phenomenal.

A sense of happiness is experienced even more powerfully when shared by many, rather than savoring it alone. This is God's intention. If the world that God created had been absolutely perfect, complete, and finished, it would be like a perfect painting, a completed work of art. There would be no need to add finishing touches, or space to alter anything.

However, God's creation is a world of energy, energy that is transmuted into various forms and develops into various phenomena. When we think of this world as a changing world of energy, how will we know when we reach the state of perfection?

Imagine a dam. If it can generate sufficient energy for the population of that region, should it be considered perfect? As a dam it is perfect, but from the perspective of the energy it contains, or of the transformation and development of that energy, the dam is not perfect if it can generate only enough power to supply energy for all the citizens. Only when it is capable of supplying unlimited energy can it be considered close to the state of perfection.

In the same way, in the world of souls and spiritual energy, the only way to say that God's creation is flawless and perfect is to provide for limitless energy. As it gushes forth, the energy must separate into many tributaries, each of which becomes as vast as the main river; this ensures an infinite supply of energy. Unless this happens, the world cannot be considered perfect. A single stream of energy is far from complete. Many tributaries must branch from the main stream of this river of energy, in turn becoming new main rivers, which again separate into many tributaries, each of which becomes a main river. Only then can this continuous flow of energy be considered perfect from the perspective of the primordial state of energy. From this we can infer the existence of God and his intention.

God's aim is to achieve boundless harmony and limitless evolution in the midst of infinite diversity and infinite individuality. Creating a society that consists of only a handful of people, being in harmony with them and making progress, is not enough. God does not set any limits on numbers. He wishes for infinite increase, achieving eternal evolution while expressing boundless harmony. As a means to this end, God invented three marvelous things.

The Three Inventions of God

Creation through Will

The most important and magnificent of God's inventions is the creation of the world by the use of will. In the beginning, God had the intention of creating the world. Human spirits, the earth, stars, rivers, and oceans were all created by God's will. In the spirit world, too, different kinds of buildings and beautiful landscapes exist; all were created using the power of the will. By will, many different things can be created. The great wisdom of the universe created the world and all the objects and phenomena in it through will.

Creation of Time

Next, God wished to place the objects created by will in the flow of time, for them to "be." For this, the invention of time was essential.

Imagine you exist in a photograph. Would you be satisfied with this two-dimensional existence? If you were photographed, your image would appear in the photo and you would certainly exist on the two-dimensional plane. But no matter how long anyone stared at the picture, it would not change; it would simply remain static.

When the world was first created, God felt very happy with his creation and he was delighted to have successfully given birth to such a variety of individuals. However, beings without movement were like pictures on a wall; seeing them every day, God gradually became dissatisfied and bored, because although these beings existed, they didn't move, develop, or transform. God felt something was missing and he wanted to add something more, so he began to think of ideas for further development. Thus, God created time.

Time is a framework for motion, a way beings can move and change. From his first invention, the law of creation using will, God came up with the ingenious idea of allowing the world to unfold of its own accord, and letting all beings develop themselves. The time lag between the first invention and the second was just a moment in earthly time. With the invention of time, beings could now change their form. Otherwise, the universe would have remained in a state of total immobility; all of us would have been static. With this great invention, the framework for motion was created. Being and time together formed the framework for development. In the flow of time, beings continue to exist while they transform themselves.

Creation of the Direction of Progress

When he saw beings freely transforming themselves of their own accord, God still felt something was missing in the fulfillment of his original intention, so he thought of giving a specific direction to the framework for motion. This gave rise to his third invention: the concepts of happiness and progress. The concepts of happiness and progress, which we can also term prosperity, are like two sides of the same coin. When God gave beings who had been endowed with motion a direction, which was progress, then they could achieve the goal of happiness.

This great universe consists of these three inventions—being, time, and progress. Within the flow of these inventions are our being and our life.

Gratitude for God's Inventions

Gratitude for Creation through Will

In the light of God's three great inventions, we must view ourselves afresh. Only then will we be aware of how great a blessing it is to come into being in this universe. We exist in the here and now as the result of a will that summons us into existence. If the creator of the universe wanted to eliminate human beings, he could make us disappear in a flash. Not only that, it would be a simple matter for him to make the entire planet disappear. It is easy for God to create and destroy, so we should be grateful and joyful that we are allowed to live each day.

With spiritual sight, you realize that animals and plants also have souls. Each flower has its own unique colors and patterns, which are the expression of an exquisite soul. Minerals are life-forms that were created before animals and plants, and they also have souls. The evolution of the souls of minerals is so slow that one year for a human being corresponds to a million or even a hundred million years for minerals. A diamond is a good example. Diamonds form from carbon deep underground that is subjected to pressure and intense heat. Volcanic activity over many centuries thrusts them closer to the surface, where they are extracted and used in the making of jewelry. The amount of time involved in all these processes is unimaginably long, but that is how mineral life is.

The transformation of carbon into a diamond is the birth of that diamond. The crystallization of a diamond equates to the birth of a human being. A diamond's life starts with its conception and follows a certain process until it is born, just as a human baby is born into this world. A newly born diamond crystal gradually increases in size, in the same way that humans grow. It then emerges to the surface of the earth to be used in various ways, in the same way that young people enter society to work. These minerals, too, have their own life history, and they possess a soul that enables them to form mineral crystals. These souls are static and motionless, but they have the power to create crystals and attract specific atoms and molecules.

It is important to understand the significance of the fact that all beings are created by the use of will. Know that no creation is accidental, but that instead every being or object exists only because there is will allowing it to be here.

Gratitude for the Creation of Time

The second invention we should be grateful for is the creation of time. Only since time was created have we been able to live; without it, we would be completely motionless, like mannequins. There would be no happiness under such conditions, so we should savor and appreciate the sense of happiness we have as a result of the existence of time.

In industrialized countries, human beings have a life span of some seventy or eighty years; this is probably the optimum length of time for our souls to evolve. The life of a dog lasts only ten or fifteen years, and some dogs even die after two or three years. A cicada lives underground for several years and has only a week aboveground. Each creature is given the appropriate life span for its spiritual development.

There is a fairy tale about a man who was able to attain immortality through some magic potion, and he was fairly happy until he got to about a hundred years old. Then his friends started to die, one after another, while he remained young for another five hundred years, then a thousand years. This story illustrates how unhappy and painful it would be if we were unable to die.

Being human, we long for eternal life, and we also want to avoid stagnation. We age and die, but there are many people who fear death. However, to be able to die after living out one's life is quite fortunate. Just as a butterfly sheds its cocoon to emerge anew, through death we are given the chance to continue our soul's development. The fact that we are given the opportunity to take a step forward is truly an enormous gift of divine compassion. Think about the greatness of this love we receive: to be allowed to incarnate again and again and to experience different lives. We are able to live only because of the invention of time, which allows our planet to exist, to revolve on its axis once every twenty-four hours, and to orbit the sun every 365 days. This is a great happiness that everyone should value and cherish.

Gratitude for the Creation of Happiness as Our Purpose

There is also a third invention that leads us to know contentment. God endowed the framework of cosmic development with a purpose, which is pursuing greater happiness. What a joy and blessing this invention is!

What if the goal of the law of motion had been depletion, destruction, extinction, or death? This world would be a very gloomy place. Selfishness can cause trouble in relationships with others, but the fact that the innermost desire of every human being, animal, and plant is to achieve a richer life is an expression of great compassion. If every life-form contained only self-destructive urges, this world would be an appalling place in which to live. The stress of civilization tends to drive humans to wage wars, but what if human souls were created with an innate desire to kill when they came of age, or with an innate tendency to destroy?

Imagine, for example, a law of nature that ordains that young people, when they reach the age of twenty, must kill their parents. A world like that might have been possible, but thanks to God, ours is not that world. Fortunately, we have the desire to move forward and develop in the direction of happiness. It goes without saying that this desire is common to people throughout the world, and we are blessed to have been created this way.

The Reincarnation of Stars and Planets

Space is also a great blessing. Thanks to the current size of the earth and the field of gravity, we are able to live in our physical bodies.

Imagine what would happen if, under enormous pressure, the earth were compressed into a ball less than one inch across, a black hole. If the size of the earth were to be reduced to little bigger than a button, all the heat and light that radiate from the earth would be sucked inward, and even the space around the earth would be distorted. We live in a three-dimensional world. In the spirit world, there are nine dimensional realms inhabited by human spirits. The ninth dimension is the highest level that a human spirit can attain; in this dimension there are currently ten spirits, each with different characteristics. Beyond this is the tenth dimension where planetary consciousnesses exist, namely the Grand Sun Consciousness, the Moon Consciousness, and the Earth Consciousness.[4]

Just as human beings repeatedly reincarnate, celestial bodies, too, experience reincarnation. As a planetary consciousness, each planet has its own soul and its own cycle of reincarnation, although the length of the cycle of reincarnation is different for each soul. The average cycle of reincarnation for a planet is approximately fifteen billion years. Within this cycle a planetary consciousness reincarnates, so at some point, a planet experiences physical death. In the course of its history, a planet can die as the result of an accident or as the consequence of a collision or of an explosion. But a planet can also die a natural death. The tenth-dimensional consciousnesses determine these cycles, and they make the necessary adjustments.

To the planetary consciousness of Earth, the globe is its physical body, consisting of a mass of large cells. Just as a human spirit resides in a physical body that after seven or eight decades goes into decline and dies, the Earth Consciousness resides in the physical planet that will eventually die. After the Earth has existed for fifteen billion years, it will begin to decay as a living entity.

When planets are about to die, they turn into black holes. Once it has fulfilled its mission, a planet with a circumference of tens of thousands of miles contracts until the circumference is less than an inch, then disintegrates and disappears. The huge planetary consciousness also becomes very small—as small as a human embryo in the mother's womb—and then enters another planet to be born anew.

There are many ways in which planets are born. Some split off from the sun, while others are created by repeated explosions through the gathering and condensation of gases and cosmic dust. A soul that has gone through the black-hole stage becomes the nucleus of this phenomenon. At this stage, the soul falls into a state of sleep and loses consciousness, exactly as a human soul does at the stage when it enters an embryo. With this soul as a nucleus, many different kinds of natural phenomena start to occur around it, such as the creation of a vortex of cosmic dust; then, a centripetal force gradually arises and begins to set off different events. As a result, a new planet is born.

Since the average cycle of reincarnation for a planet is about fifteen billion years, Earth will likely continue to exist for quite a while before dying a natural death.

The Principle of Salvation: What to Tell Others

To understand the principle of salvation, it is important to understand the nature of the universe and of human existence. Unless we grasp these fundamentals, we lose ground in our efforts to convey the Truth.

What is the purpose of spreading the Truth? Is it to advertise the name of our organization, so that we can have the satisfaction of increasing our numbers? Or is there a greater purpose? We need to clearly understand all of these fundamental issues before we can proceed with concrete plans of action.

Existence Is the Creation of God

What is critical to convey to others, including those who are ignorant of the Truth, and even those with no desire to know of the existence of God and the soul? Before anything else, we must tell them of God's first invention: the creation of the universe, human beings, and all life through his will. We need to put this first Truth into our own words and then share it with others. Those who don't know how this world came into being tend to have a materialistic view of life, and believe that life on earth is merely accidental. They think they were thrown randomly into this world, born by chance into a random environment. They believe that death is the end of everything. However, this view of life clearly contradicts the Truth that has been revealed and taught throughout human history. If these people are going to change their views of life, they will need to have the Truth explained in a way they can understand.

Only when we realize that essentially we are all part of God's creation can we nurture each other and awaken to genuine gratitude. As long as people view life as the by-product of an accident, there is no space for appreciation or happiness to arise out of interactions with others. This is why it is important to begin by explaining God's first invention in your own words.

The existence of the soul and the body is an extension of this first Truth. The world of matter was created, and is maintained, through the transformation of spiritual energy. Everything in this phenomenal world unfolds as an extension of God's first invention.

The Meaning of Time

Next, it is essential to tell others about God's second invention, the meaning of time. Time has two meanings. The first gives context to our individual lives. We need to inform people how best to use the time we are given in this life, and how to create time that encompasses the value of Truth.

In my book *Love, Nurture, and Forgive,*[5] I spoke of the two different types of time in which we live—"relative time" and "absolute time." Relative time refers to time that can be measured objectively by a clock. If I talk in public for an hour, one hour elapses for every listener. However, depending on how much Truth a person digests and assimilates in that one hour, a lifetime can expand infinitely. For some people, such an enlightening experience is the equivalent of living in eternity. This sort of time, which contains the value of Truth, is absolute time.

This reflects Einstein's theory of relativity in relation to the Truth, wherein both relative time and absolute time exist. It is the law of physics applied to the realm of Truth.

The second meaning of time has to do with the significance of the era in which we live. We really need to understand the significance of our present era in the context of the long history of humankind and go beyond living humdrum lives. We are standing at the very turning point of an epoch. In the face of worldly misfortune and confusion, it is urgent that we convey the Truth to others. The high spirits in heaven are in a hurry, and we must be, too.

If you don't understand the significance of these times in which you are living, you may be oblivious. I want to publish many books of Truth as quickly as possible, because the torch of Dharma must be lit before a much more difficult age arrives. We are hurrying to build the foundations, make them solid, and spread the Truth. You are alive at a crucial turning point for humankind.

Happiness as Our Goal

Finally, we must pursue God's third invention faithfully: the goal of happiness. Humankind's goal is not the survival of only a handful of people, nor is it the survival of a single nation or culture. From the very beginning, we have been expected to embrace all kinds of individuality and diversity and to pursue infinite happiness through the expression of universal harmony and evolution. Without happiness, there can be no salvation.

The movement for salvation must include these three aspects: the power that allows all beings to exist, the creation of time, and the goal of happiness. With these ideas as our foundation, we can move forward to create an ideal world.

NINE

The Principle of
Self-Reflection

What Is Self-Reflection?

Happy Science began the movement to spread the Truth with the publication of books of the Truth. It is growing to become a great force that will, in due course, influence the whole world.

The Truth has been stated in a multitude of ways, and as you study it, you may find it difficult to recognize where you actually stand in relation to it. At this stage it is crucial that you concentrate on establishing the self.* Once we begin to feel the breath of development, we must return to the self, look deeply within, and build the inner strength that will support further steps and progress.

In my book *The Essence of Buddha,* I described in plain language the thoughts of Shakyamuni Buddha, who lived in India 2,600 years ago. I may reveal the details of his eighty-one years of life in another book, but to begin with, I have condensed his life's teachings to present the basic framework of Buddhism. Even if you have read numerous Buddhist scriptures, you cannot claim to have grasped the essence of Buddhist teachings until you have understood the contents of this

_____
*You must establish your own self before you are able to save others successfully.

book. What did the Buddha want to convey? Simply put, the message contained in *The Essence of Buddha* is "Understand the importance of self-reflection."

You may wonder why we practice self-reflection and what its purpose is. You may ask yourself, "Do we practice it just because it is considered to be good or does the act of self-reflection have some deeper meaning?"

I have been given the ability to see, hear, and know things that most people cannot. I must tell you that although you may believe that you lead an independent, self-determined life and have control over almost 100 percent of your own thoughts and actions, this is not necessarily the case. You must accept the possibility that you are being manipulated like a puppet.

Many events are unfolding in the invisible world, and the spiritual influences from those events affect whether we can lead happy lives. Although so many people—more than six billion—now live on this earth, most are unaware of being under some kind of negative spiritual influence. In fact, very few are under the direct guidance of their guardian and guiding spirits.*

Most people are exposed to negative vibrations at certain times of the day, although for how long, and to what extent, differs from person to person. It is very sad that as children of God we live in such miserable conditions. Human beings are regarded as the greatest of all earthly creatures; nevertheless, they are influenced by animal spirits, or spirits who have gone astray. Many people become trapped in a life they never envisioned, suffering negative consequences and bearing the responsibility for those consequences. Whenever I see people who have allowed their lives to be influenced by the ill will of these spirits, and as a result have fallen into a spiritual abyss, I am all the more determined to eliminate such negative influences so that people can live their lives to the fullest every single day.

---

*Guiding spirits assist people who have a great mission in fulfilling it.

Why do you allow yourself to be misled by these negative influences? Awaken immediately to the truth that you are a child of God; it is time to let your divine nature shine forth. The way to achieve this is through self-reflection, the importance of which has been taught since ancient times.

The Threefold Path of La Mu

As we indicated earlier, about seventeen thousand years ago, on the ancient continent known as Mu, there was a great emperor by the name of La Mu. He taught his people the importance of practicing self-reflection, saying, "Restore your true self. To achieve this, eliminate negative materialistic vibrations and dispel all anxiety from your mind."

From ancient times, numerous high spirits have come down to earth to teach and guide people living in many different circumstances. Through all of these eras, there has been one immutable teaching: "With the power of your own will, correct your errors. Only when you have done this will the grand river of destiny flow in the direction you wish." One way to correct errors is the Eightfold Path, taught by Shakyamuni Buddha. La Mu taught a different way, which I call the Threefold Path.

The first step in La Mu's Threefold Path was self-reflection on love. La Mu taught, "Human beings should live always loving others, so reflect every day on whether or not you have given love to others."

The second teaching was "Reflect on your day today and see whether or not you were able to attune your mind to God, and to your guardian and guiding spirits who are closer to God." He taught, "If you are unable to hear the voice of your guardian and guiding spirits, either directly or indirectly, it is because clouds are covering your mind, obstructing these voices.* If the compass needle of your mind doesn't

_____

*Originally the mind is pure, but when one has thoughts that go against the mind of God, such as anger, resentment, and jealousy, clouds form over the mind and obstruct God's light.

point to the heavenly world, the cause must lie in your thoughts and actions during the day. Therefore, reflect upon your thoughts and actions."

The third of La Mu's teachings was "Reflect on what you have learned during this day. Check and see that you have not wasted the day. Life lasts only a matter of decades, and to be born on this earth into the circumstances you are now experiencing is a rare opportunity. Only those blessed with extremely good fortune are born in an age when the Truth is being taught. Do not waste this lifetime. Do not waste this year. Do not waste this day. Use all your experiences as material for learning. Do not finish a day without having learned from it. Do not let an hour, a minute, or even a second go by without learning from it."

You may think that the Noble Eightfold Path is the definitive method of self-reflection. But the starting point of self-reflection lies in the strong resolution not to waste the time that is given to each one of us in this lifetime. If you hold to this as the essence of reflective self-examination, you can practice it in many different ways.

I teach the "True" Eightfold Path, which reinterprets the traditional Noble Eightfold Path in the context of modern life so that everyone can understand what Shakyamuni actually taught. However, this is not the only method of self-reflection; there are many different methods, appropriate for varying levels of development and spiritual understanding. I recommend La Mu's Threefold Path as a simple way to begin the practice of self-reflection. Since there are only three criteria to check, it should be relatively easy to begin to practice right away.

First, see if you gave love to others today. Human beings are born to give love. Not giving love goes against your true nature.

Second, reflect on the harmony of your mind. If you are unable to communicate with your guardian and guiding spirits, it is because the vibration of your mind is disturbed. So calm the vibration of your mind and make a daily effort to maintain inner serenity.

Third, reflect on whether you learned as much as you could today. This aspect of self-reflection creates a more positive self.

Many people think that self-reflection is simply the process of looking back on the past, but the true purpose of self-reflection is to correct, and learn from, your mistaken thoughts and actions, thereby creating a more constructive life. More than simply discovering past mistakes and making up for them, like resetting a negative reading to zero, the ultimate objective of self-reflection is the development of a more positive self, and the realization of a utopia on earth as the fulfillment of God's will. This is the point at which we can no longer differentiate between self-reflection and prayer. We should not concentrate solely on the method and lose sight of the intention. The essence of self-reflection can be reduced to a single statement: We should try to correct ourselves and develop a more positive self, so that we can make a greater contribution to society.

Self-reflection involves some complicated elements, and often its effects may not be obvious. Very few people really understand the remarkable power of self-reflection. With spiritual sight, I can see that the moment someone begins to reflect, he is lifted away from the negative spiritual influences that have held him back, as if restraining ropes have been severed.

Manifesting Divine Nature Within

Many people think that light comes from a higher power that is outside of us, and that the light from this outside power grants us salvation. This notion contains some truth. When you recite the prayers in our Prayer Books, you become a spiritual source emitting spiritual energy or vibrations, creating a golden bridge that connects you to the realms of the high spirits. By means of this bridge, guiding spirits give you power.

However, this is not the only aspect of divine light. One reason I chose to talk about the practice of self-reflection prior to talking about the practice of prayer is to make it clear that light does not always come from outside. The essence of the self-reflection that Shakyamuni taught is that "light emanates from within."

Those who attended meditation seminars at Happy Science and practiced the Meditation on Happiness have probably experienced the Meditation on the Full Moon.* This full moon meditation is not a simple meditation practice; it represents the ultimate state that can be achieved through self-reflection. When I practice self-reflection, I look into my inner self, going deeply into my mind, and I find an image of myself. It's not a physical body, but something like a golden statue of Buddha. Light emanates from the statue, especially from the lower abdomen. This reflective state, reachable through the full moon meditation, is actually the perfected state of self-reflection. When you practice self-reflection, examine each individual thought that passes through your mind, and then you will enter a state of deep concentration. However, your practice of self-reflection is not complete until you can imagine light radiating from your whole body. This light is called an aura, or halo, and it is not merely a physical phenomenon. To spiritual sight, your body looks like a golden statue emanating an intense light in all directions. This is a different light from the light you receive in the act of praying. That light comes from high above, whereas the light that comes from self-reflection radiates from within. Once you have this knowledge, you will be able to understand the structure of the mind.

The human mind is multilayered, like an onion. The fourth through tenth dimensions form layers, one inside the other. Once you experience the light that radiates from within, you will become conscious of these layers.

At the center of the human mind is the core, which is connected to the Real World and even to the world that is beyond the realm of human spirits. The ninth dimension is the highest sphere where individual human spirits exist,† but within us there is a part that receives light from the tenth dimension, and even beyond. It is important to

---

*The full moon meditation, which has been practiced since the time of Shakyamuni, is a meditation in which the mind is harmonized by visualizing the full moon.
†The highest realm from which a spirit in the terrestrial spirit group can take human form is the ninth dimension.

know how to seek this light from within. The deepest, most profound part of our mind is connected to the Supreme Consciousness that exists in the deepest recesses of the great universe.

Here lies the central teaching of Shakyamuni Buddha. We can make a clear distinction between the teachings of the two great spiritual teachers, Jesus Christ and Shakyamuni Buddha, on this very point. Jesus perceived the Absolute, who transcends human beings and exists far beyond; he sometimes referred to this being as "Father" and at other times as "God." Jesus understood and taught that there is a transcendental existence far greater than the human soul dwelling in a physical body. This is the starting point of faith in an outside power.*

Shakyamuni did not teach of an outside power. He did not regard human beings on earth, or souls that dwell in physical bodies, as weak. Humans appear to be frail, and some Christians believe themselves to be sinners. Jesus did not teach that human beings are sinners.† In the eyes of Shakyamuni, human beings are truly powerful, with a strong inner core. Of course, he had seen people swayed by the currents of destiny and caught in the vortex of karma. He observed many fragile people, just as Jesus did, but Shakyamuni recognized God's light at the core of every person. So he did not consider faith to be reverence toward something far away. Rather, his teaching was "Awaken to the light within, your inner core. There you can find everything. There you can see everything and receive all power."[1] In his view of the world, the inner universe embraces the outer. Only through this perspective does the act of faith transform itself into a more powerful energy.

The inner self and the outer transcendental consciousness do not exist separately; they have the same source. Those who have fully awakened to this fact can be truly strong and live with vigor and courage. The teachings of Buddhism can be reduced to a single tenet: "Stop asking for outside help to try to escape, in the belief that you are weak.

---

*Religions that emphasize faith in an outside power tend to believe that one can attain happiness and be saved by devotion to this outside power alone.
†Some Christians believe that they are born into sin, and can be forgiven only by God.

You are not weak. Buddha lives within you. Behold the Buddha within and awaken to his existence. Manifest the Buddha-nature that is within your own mind." Until you understand this truth, you cannot claim to understand Buddhism. Your challenge is to go deeply into the mind to discover this inner light, the fire within.

The True Eightfold Path

Right View

In the Eightfold Path, Right View comes first. This means checking whether you are seeing things rightly or fairly, without bias. This may appear to be a simple task, but how many people actually ask themselves whether or not they are viewing things correctly?

There are three checkpoints for Right View. The first is your perspective of the people around you. The majority of human suffering comes from personal relationships, so check whether you are seeing others and their state of being correctly. Right View means seeing things in exactly the same way as God would see them. Check and see whether your views match the image of the world that is reflected in the mirror of God's mind.

Another checkpoint is the way you see yourself. Check whether you were too easy on yourself today, if you viewed yourself with a bias, and if your estimation of yourself was either too high or too low. Did you evaluate yourself in the reflection of God's mind or did you use only your own criteria to justify yourself? This practice leads you to see yourself accurately.

The third checkpoint is your perspective of your interactions with others. Many daily events occur as a result of people living and working interdependently. Check and see whether you observed these events rightly. See if you had a fair perspective on what happened during the day, or on every incident that occurred around you.

Only through practicing this self-reflection will the Buddha-nature, the divine nature that has been dormant within you, gradually awaken.

As your practice of Right View deepens, you will begin to view others differently. You will be able to distinguish clearly between the "I"—a manifestation of their ego—and their true divine nature. When I view people, I'm not looking at a human form wearing clothes, but seeing the light of Buddha that is within each person. What I see is to what extent each person is manifesting his or her true nature as a child of God, and how that light shines forth. A person's external appearance is not important. It is just a fleeting image, like the images of a film that are projected onto a screen, appearing and disappearing without a trace. What I really want to see, and truly want to know, is the part of you that never changes in the midst of this ever-changing life. That is your Buddha-nature.

Right Speech

Another important practice of the Eightfold Path is Right Speech. This is difficult to practice, yet is the most obvious checkpoint for self-reflection. It is so difficult to practice that we cannot master Right Speech in just one or two years. Controlling our words requires tremendous effort, but human society is founded on words.

Self-Reflection on Right Speech is not limited to spoken words. It includes written words and body language, which sometimes expresses your thoughts more eloquently than any words. Your facial expressions and eyes are more articulate than your lips. The subtleties of your eyes and face express your feelings more than what comes out of your mouth. Self-reflection on Right Speech includes all body language.

The Real World is a world of thought. In that world, thoughts and actions are not separate, but are one and the same. Everything you think, be it good or bad, manifests immediately. On earth, however, your thoughts do not always produce direct results; they are manifested through your words and actions. For this reason, you must be conscious of your words.

Typical spirits in hell never speak a word in favor of the happiness of others, only of their own. They don't realize that the words they utter defile themselves as well as their divine nature.

Words are fascinating; they teach us more clearly than anything else whether or not we are living in accordance with God's will. If you find it difficult to practice deep reflection, think about the words you speak. Try to imagine what the world of angels would be like. There can be no heaven where people harm each other with words.

To put it another way, heaven is created with words. The spirits in hell have no physical body and they exist as thoughts. If they want to change hell into heaven, they need to correct their words; once they do, a heavenly world will immediately unfold. It's that simple. Many people are unable to practice Right Speech, and that is why the underworld exists.

There are no limits to Right Speech. Ultimately, Right Speech must be composed of words of Truth that possess the strongest and most refined spiritual power. You haven't completed self-reflection on Right Speech simply because you've said nothing to harm others. You must deepen your reflection and examine how many words of Truth you could have offered to others but didn't. Many people feel content once they have finished checking whether or not they uttered hurtful words, but self-reflection goes beyond that. How many words of Truth did you convey to the people you met? Were you able to give nourishment to their souls and kindle a light in their hearts? You must always check these points when you practice self-reflection.

Right Livelihood

The third path of the Eightfold Path is Right Livelihood, or leading one's life rightly. The original meaning of Right Livelihood is "to fulfill one's life purpose."*[2] What does fulfilling one's life purpose mean? It means to allow our souls, which are thrust into this world of time and space, to manifest their original state.

Looking back on the twenty-four hours of a day, there might be times when you think you've done well, but did you live these twenty-four hours in accordance with God's will? Is it possible that someone

---

*A way to reflect on the fulfillment of your life purpose is to imagine how you will feel at the time of death.

else who has awakened to the Truth more deeply would have used those same hours more effectively? Ask yourself these questions, and you will realize that self-reflection on Right Livelihood is never ending. Right Livelihood means the most effective use of the time you are given in this life.

This is not the time measured by a clock, where one hour is the same for everyone, but the absolute value of time, when one is living in accordance with the Truth. That time has a different spiritual value for each of us. From the perspective of the Truth, an hour spent by one person may not be worth a minute or even a second for another, and that same one hour can be worth a thousand years to someone else. For those who listened to a sermon of Jesus, the worth of that one hour might have been two thousand years in terms of the absolute value.

How much time have you lived as your truly awakened self? Most people may feel content when they consider how efficiently and effectively they spend their time. However, when you ask yourself whether you are able to live one day in such a way that it is worth an entire lifetime, or even a thousand or two thousand years, you will realize that there is infinite room for improvement.

Right Action

The next path in the Eightfold Path is Right Action, or Right Work. For those who have a profession of some kind, this checkpoint may appear similar to Right Livelihood.

However, have you ever considered the significance of your work, whether it be in an office, a factory, outdoors, or at home? Most people spend at least a third of their lifetime working, once they become contributing members of society. It's easy to become absorbed in the daily routine and never question why you are working. Are you satisfied using your time merely to earn a living? Is getting paid your only motivation for working? Suppose your life were to end today and you were to look back on your entire life. Could you say your work was what you really wanted to do? At work, did you exert yourself to the fullest, or do you feel you could have done more? Could you say you worked with all your heart and soul?

Your work is important in two respects. First, it is the starting point for building an ideal world on earth. It is important to know that through your work you can make changes in society and in the environment around you.

Second, your occupation provides you with the raw material for expanding your enlightenment. Work provides you with the opportunity to practice the second stage of love, spiritually nurturing love. Your relationships with people in the workplace are valuable learning experiences. You should appreciate the fact that you are given the chance to raise and intensify your enlightenment through work.

Through work, there are infinite ways of nurturing others spiritually. If you are a company president, for example, you may be responsible for supporting tens of thousands of employees.

However, your success and development through work must not be limited to merely benefiting these employees. Instead, go beyond the limits of your company and search constantly for opportunities to exert an influence on a national or even an international level. There are infinite possibilities for expanding the field of influence of spiritually nurturing love. These possibilities increase your spiritual strength and develop a generous spirit.

In addition to the level of the soul's spiritual awareness, which is represented by enlightenment, the soul has breadth, which is expressed in its capacity to embrace others. Even with a limited level of enlightenment, someone still can have a great capacity for generosity and acceptance. Only by practicing spiritually nurturing love on many different occasions is it possible to develop the capacity to embrace and guide diverse people.

Right Thought

The first four practices of the Eightfold Path are of great importance for those who have decided to pursue spiritual development. Right Thought requires a stricter discipline than the previous four practices, and is crucial for those who are more serious about pursuing enlightenment and devoting themselves to daily self-discipline. Right View, Right Speech, Right Livelihood, and Right Action are concrete practical checkpoints that are relatively easy to practice. Many people may find Right Thought more difficult. How deeply you are able to explore the path of Right Thought reveals how genuinely, how seriously you are seeking enlightenment.

The nature of the mind is ever changing. To my eyes, sometimes its form is kaleidoscopic; at others, it resembles a round ball. The mind can contract to a tiny point, and it can expand infinitely to encompass the entire universe. Because there is virtually no end to exploring Right Thought, we reincarnate again and again for eternity, until we have completely understood it.

My books provide material to help you study the Truth so that you can truly understand Right Thought. Your inner world is multifaceted and complex. The study of the Truth gives you the knowledge to examine this world from every angle.

Right Effort

What enhances and supports your practice of Right Thought is Right Effort—making a focused effort in the right direction. Human beings are essentially equal, but there are those who are proceeding in the direction of God and those going in the opposite direction.

Turn toward God. This is the first step toward happiness. If your direction is wrong from the outset, no matter how diligent your efforts, they are in vain. So face the right direction and go forward on the right path step-by-step—that is Right Effort.

The objective of Right Effort is to attain enlightenment. If you don't set this goal, you cannot claim you are making Right Effort. Each person has a different spiritual level and lives in a different environment, but without exception, you cannot achieve Right Effort unless you wish to discover enlightenment. For this you require a strong will, courage, vigor, and a sense of responsibility.

You may claim that you live rightly on a daily basis, but do you pass each day without any ideals or sense of purpose, like a reed floating on the water? If so, put down strong roots and grow straight toward the sky. This is what Right Effort is all about. Even if you feel content to stay in a pure environment, like a reed floating in the clean water of an aquarium, this is not the true purpose of life. Do not be satisfied with seeking purity of mind alone; that is not the limit of your spiritual growth. Aim for something greater. Develop and grow like a giant tree. Only when you endeavor to grow in this way can you truly be called a child of God, one within whom divine nature dwells.

Right Mindfulness

The last two paths of the Eightfold Path are Right Mindfulness and Right Concentration. These practices mark an advanced level of spiritual discipline. After you have cleared the hurdles of Right Mindfulness and Right Concentration, you will have reached the first stage at which you can be called an "awakened one," or an Arhat. At this level, a spiritual light, or halo, will appear around your head, and you will be able to receive messages from your guardian spirit. You are approaching the stage where you can give light to others. In order to reach this first stage of enlightenment, Right Mindfulness and Right Concentration are indispensable. Right Mindfulness refers not to the thoughts and ideas that flow in everyday life, but rather to the direction of a strong will projected far into the future.

The power of will in Right Mindfulness is like a locomotive engine, pulling Right Effort forward. "The power of will" here doesn't mean simply planning a course of action; it also includes the thoughts directed toward our guardian and guiding spirits, what we call prayers. Thoughts that are transmitted with a specific purpose are willpower. So Right Mindfulness also involves prayers to God and the high spirits who are close to him.

Right Mindfulness can also include prayers to correct your path or prayers of gratitude. It can be a sparkling joy at having been blessed with life or a clear vision of a bright future. Our minds send out many thoughts. Even though we live in this three-dimensional world of length, width, and height, we can transcend this third dimension by embracing the multidimensional world within, and through Right Mindfulness. By sending the power of the will forth in all directions, we can build a bridge from this world to the Real World. It is a way for us to transcend our three-dimensional world on earth and move closer to God.

Right Concentration

Finally there is Right Concentration, or meditating rightly. There are many kinds of meditation, including reflective meditation, in which you clear the clouds that cover your mind, and visualization meditation.

Meditation also includes the state in which your mind is constantly connected to the world of high spirits through prayer. Through Right Concentration, we can come to experience true liberation of the soul while still living in this world. When we feel that our minds no longer belong to this world but transcend it, we have completed Right Concentration. Only through this experience can we become free from the restrictions of our physical bodies and this material world and find the true self, a being belonging to higher dimensions. This is one of the final objectives of self-reflection.

Self-Reflection is a way to discover the true self* while still living in this world, to live a life of Truth and discover the magnificent self within, the self that is connected to higher dimensions. If you do not pass through the gate of self-reflection, you will never know enlightenment.

---

*The true self is the self that manifests divine nature, the core of the self that is a child of God.

TEN

The Principle of Prayer

The Spiritual Power of Words of Truth

Finally we come to the last principle, the principle of prayer. We have already covered the principle of self-reflection, but when we think of God, the elements of prayer and self-reflection are both essential.

Starting with the principle of happiness, I have described the principles of love, the mind, enlightenment, progress, wisdom, utopia, salvation, and self-reflection. These comprise the framework of my philosophy.

In this last chapter, I discuss the principle of prayer, a vital step in developing knowledge of the Truth and building a bridge that leads to God. No matter how much intellectual study of the Truth you may have undertaken, if you haven't finally awakened to faith and the love for God, the bulk of your efforts will not bear fruit.

You are born into this three-dimensional world to grow through various experiences, and to acquire some knowledge on a range of subjects. You are given many opportunities to awaken to the Truth. Through those experiences, you are expected to come to a true understanding of God's will, and to live accordingly. There must be no compromise in this endeavor—the Truth cannot be distorted by human thought or worldly knowledge. Eternal Truth is immortal, continuing to shine through past, present, and future and piercing hundreds of millions of years of space and time.

My mission is to reveal the Truth, immutable in the eternal flow of time. If I were unable to understand and teach this, my present incarnation would be meaningless, and I would rather not live this life. I am determined to convey the Truth created by God for all eternity, and to summon the hearts of all to God's will, to the power and energy that pour forth from the divine. Otherwise, there is no point in having founded Happy Science, or in developing it further.

What is your purpose in learning the Truth? What do you expect to learn from this book? Some of you have purchased books of the Truth, and others listen to recordings of my lectures. Why are you searching for the Truth?

I don't give lectures and seminars simply for idle purposes. Above all else, I want people to realize the significance of our present era. When books of Truth share shelf space with countless others, it is difficult to perceive their differentiating qualities of light and energy. That is why I give lectures and address people directly, so as to reveal the true quality of that light. The lectures I give are mine, but at the same time, they are not. You listen to me, but at the same time, it is not Ryuho Okawa you hear.

What is the source of the vibration, energy, and light of my words? It is the most authoritative source you could possibly imagine, an energy you cannot experience directly even in the other world. You have the opportunity to connect with that energy at this very moment. Words such as these, from beyond the human sphere, have not been heard since Jesus Christ left the earth two thousand years ago, nor has this spiritual power been experienced on earth.

Be Pure in Heart

Self-Reflection and Prayer

In the preceding chapter on the practice of self-reflection, you learned how to look directly at the inner self, bare your heart and mind, and, in this clarity, see God. Through this practice, you come to recall long forgotten feelings.

The ideal and eternal world of liberation doesn't exist in some far-away place that is completely separate from you, but in the heart of each individual. To practice self-reflection is to know the true mind. Thoughts that start in self-reflection soar higher and higher, without any limits, as well as to the depths of the inner world. What starts from within soars into a far distant, multidimensional world where we have our origin.

No matter how eagerly I may wish to communicate how it feels to encounter high dimensional beings and the world to which they belong, it's simply not possible. The world of higher dimensions is beyond description.

Once you witness its sublime and powerful beauty, your understanding of this earthly world will be completely changed. You will step into a world where you are no longer on earth, yet are still living here; you are no longer a physical being, yet you still have a human body.

You can achieve this through prayer, but it isn't easy. When we become enmeshed in the vibrations of the third dimension, our prayers tend to become distorted and, at times, reach completely unexpected worlds. As someone who teaches prayer, I have to remind people sternly of the truth about praying, which angels in the other world would like everyone on this earth to know: No matter how hard you pray, there are times when your prayers do not reach heaven. It is an undeniable fact that a certain set of laws governs the world of prayer. You must learn these laws.

The Laws of Prayer

There are certain conditions for prayer. Above all else, you must be pure in heart. I usually recommend first practicing self-reflection, then meditation, and finally prayer. But if you want to begin with prayer, your heart must first be pure. Unless this first step is fulfilled, your prayer will not reach heaven. This is the law, because the world where prayers are received is a world of pure hearts. Praying is like making a telephone call; it is the act of connecting lines of thought. It directs the compass needle of the mind toward the heavenly world.

The world beyond this earth is a world where only thoughts exist. In order for your prayers to attune to that world, you must send out the kind of thoughts that correspond to that world. In Buddhist teachings, being pure is often expressed as "removing attachment." But I will simply say, "Be pure in heart."

Every day you meet a wide range of people. How often do you meet people who impress you with their purity of heart? As you examine yourself, can you confidently declare that you have been living with a pure heart? In the process of living, your mind becomes entangled in various thoughts that engender negativity.

Purity of heart means experiencing moments when you become transparent, as if the self has disappeared. Sometimes when you look back at your day, you may be surprised to find that your thoughts have been focused entirely on yourself, and may have consisted entirely of concerns about your own happiness or unhappiness.

Can you discover any "transparent" moments where the "I" disappeared? Was your mind full of sentences that did not begin with "I" as the subject? When you enter the world of prayer, your sentences do not need a subject. "I" or "he," "human" or "God"—these kinds of words become unnecessary. You must become one with the energy that runs through the entire universe. This is the only requirement for genuine prayer.

To this end, be infinitely pure and transparent and radiate brilliance. Rather than feeling love to get something for yourself, feel love for its own sake. Rather than feeling love for others, feel love for the sake of love itself. Love on account of love; love because love is a joy. Rejoice simply because rejoicing is a joy. Put these words into practice and enjoy this state to the fullest. Rather than praying for some purpose, discover prayer for its own sake, the pure act of praying. If you are pure in heart, enjoy this purity. Appreciate it not for yourself or for anyone else, but simply for itself.

Experiencing Oneness with God

When you are able to reach this state, your mind will be transparent. Your thoughts will be purified and eventually transcend all objectives. "What for?" and "For whom?" will no longer be relevant. Your prayers will be purified, and you will experience a state of oneness with God. In that very moment is the greatest possible happiness for a human being. In Buddhist terms, it is enlightenment, where there is no distinction between the mind of God and the mind of the self. Ideally, of course, we should maintain this state constantly, but it's difficult for ordinary mortals. So take a few moments every day to experience oneness with God.

I am extremely grateful to be able to live in a state of complete oneness with divinity twenty-four hours a day, because I have no desire to live for my own sake. There may be times when I appear to be leading an ordinary life, but I have no intention of living for myself. In order that I may serve as the foundation for something greater, I sublimate myself, becoming selfless and transparent. Those who live out their days in a state of total oneness with God no longer suffer or have personal worries.

You probably have your own unique personal problems, those you believe to be different from the difficulties of others. However, the very fact that you have any worries at all indicates that you have not yet attained a state of oneness with God. The greater, deeper, and more diverse your suffering, the more you need to develop spiritually, since your suffering indicates that you are still living within the confines of the tiny world of trial and error.

The Nature of True Prayer

A Passion to Bring Happiness to All Humankind

In order to experience true prayer, to actually experience oneness with God, it is important to unload everyday worries and distress. Unless you solve these problems, you cannot attune your mind to the mind of God.

I can almost hear you saying, "But I've never met anyone who doesn't worry." You may think it's only natural to continually suffer.

In this case I would advise the reverse: Spend time worrying, but at least consider the nature of your worries and make them of a higher quality. Ask yourself if you would feel embarrassed for others to see the issues that worry you. You may be exaggerating trifling concerns that really don't merit your time. If you are going to worry, do it seriously, on behalf of God.

It is important to have a higher quality of worry, and also to adopt a broader perspective. Once you begin to worry on God's behalf, you will understand the true nature of the worries that have been weighing on your mind. You may be worrying about something as minuscule as a mustard seed, or even tinier. You have more important things to worry about, but because you are unaware of them, you magnify trivial concerns and rush around in a state of confusion.

If you are going to worry, have the kind of worries God would have. If God worries at all, it is probably more like a passion to improve the world and to bring light and happiness into it. It is important to transform your worries into this kind of passion. When you look at your inner world from the grand perspective of passion, you will feel the worries that possess you drop away, one after another. Your worrying indicates only that you have not yet awakened to a superior mission, a sublime passion. People cannot focus on two things at once—this is a truth as well as a psychological law. So change what is in your mind; fill it with something entirely different—the passion to bring happiness to all people. This is the best way to become worry-free. Anyone with a knitted brow, looking anxious and making a lot of fuss over nothing, can experience a moment of sudden transformation and become someone who radiates a brilliant light. Awakening to this moment is the first step to holy prayer.

The Narrow Gate of Prayer

If you ever think about learning the principle of prayer in an attempt to fulfill some selfish desire, get rid of that notion. That sort of thought has already closed the gateway to prayer, the entrance to oneness with God.

To become one with the divine, or to enter the royal road to success, you must discard all that is unnecessary or trivial. Those wishing to learn how to pray to achieve some small ambition are not able to pass through the gateway of prayer, or even to stand in front of that gate.

Large numbers of angels stand just beyond the gate of prayer. The moment you pass through the gate, you will face the angels. In your current state of mind, with your current attitudes, could you face this audience? Would you not feel ashamed to show yourself and reveal your thoughts before them?

This is not about the need for self-reflection, or even repentance. After some years or decades, each one of you, without exception, will leave your physical body and return to the other world. At that moment, when you stand before the angels, how will you feel when you become aware of how trivial the desires behind your thoughts and actions have been? You will realize that you cannot stand before the angels as you are; their presence will be too dazzling. The light of angels makes you feel as if you are disappearing, almost fading away. Dazzled by this light, you can no longer think, or hold on to any desire. You will experience this state of being as a reality at some point. But by praying, you can get a glimpse of it at this very moment.

Entering the world of prayer means you are already dead to your physical body, which houses the soul. In that moment, you are as good as dead to the three-dimensional world, but the realms of the fourth dimension and beyond come to life.

If you read other books of mine, you will understand that while those living on earth perceive death as an abhorrent event that brings grief and agony, the inhabitants of the Real World believe that what we call "life" in this world *is* a kind of death. Perhaps death is too strong a description, but it is at least true that people living on earth grope blindly. They are unable to see the Truth, unable to act as they truly want, and don't understand God's wishes or those of their guardian and guiding spirits. In this fumbling, blind life, they mistakenly believe that they are enjoying freedom to the fullest.

The Real World sees this life not as freedom, but merely as a state where people crawl around trying to grasp at whatever their hands touch, unable to see or hear the Truth. Nevertheless, those living on earth mistakenly consider themselves to be enjoying a state of freedom and expressing their individuality.

The Real World sees this as completely absurd, a far cry from true freedom. Just as a newborn baby lacks freedom, to the spirit world we are all newborns, even though we are adults. In moments of self-reflection or in prayer, which is a deeper state than self-reflection, we leave this world for an instant to return to the world from which we originally came. In these moments, we return to our original state of ultimate freedom.

Being Reborn through Prayer

We see prayer as a bridge that connects us to God and high spirits. In Real World terms, it is an act of reawakening to eternal life. It is the moment when we reveal our true self to the sun of the Truth. For those on earth, the moment of prayer is both a death and a rebirth. If we are born again through prayer, we can no longer continue to live as we did before. If, after prayer, we continue to live in the same way, with the same mind-set we had previously, what was the point of dying and coming back to life? If the act of prayer is reincarnation experienced in a moment, then in that moment, some transformation must occur within us.

Prayer is the effort to transform the self. Prayers said merely for your own benefit or to get a financial windfall are not truly prayers. Such so-called prayers have been offered time and again for hundreds and thousands of years, and have always been rejected in the name of Truth. A true prayer is a rebirth. The moment we glimpse the Real World, we cannot help but be born anew. Through this experience a human being can experience rebirth within one lifetime.

The moment you pray to God, your present life is completely cut off from the past. If you have not been spiritually transformed by praying, your prayer might have unintended consequences. It could very well turn into a sword that attacks you. This is what happens when prayers are used for selfish ends.

The Purification of the Earth

What Happens to Misguided Prayers

Prayer works according to the laws of energy. Any wish that takes the form of a prayer will be heard by other beings, even if it does not reach God. It may be heard by the inhabitants of hell, who also listen to the thoughts and wishes of those on earth. Sometimes they give people a "helping hand," an act of convoluted "kindness." Those who receive help from such beings gradually become captive to them, thus contributing to an increase in the dark energy of hellish thoughts.

Mistaken prayers can be a source of energy for the inhabitants of hell, an indescribably miserable realm. While the spirits in heaven receive energy directly from the spiritual sun, the spirits in hell are blocked from absorbing its energy by dense clouds of negative thought. However, these spirits are also subject to the laws of energy. Their energy comes from negative thoughts generated by human beings on earth, most of which are the result of wrong desires, including prayers for selfish intentions.

When you pray you must seek God seriously, as if you are standing on the edge of a cliff that separates life from death. Let your devotion leap toward God. Praying without this kind of resolve will have the completely opposite effect—your prayers will sustain spirits in hell.

Negative energy makes these spirits stronger and more active, enabling them to pull people on earth further in the wrong direction. It is a kind of vicious cycle. Once you become aware of this cycle, you must end it at all costs.

The Dissolution of Hell

It's easy to say that we must banish hell. Some people may even question why God and high spirits in heaven don't eliminate it altogether. In the current circumstances, however, hell cannot be eliminated without destroying this earthly world. Would you choose to dissolve this earthly world in order to get rid of hell?

Eliminating this world would result in the total eradication of

God's hope for its prosperity, development, and evolution. Although this world was originally created for the evolution and development of humankind, it is becoming a source and a stronghold of evil. Knowing this truth, would you destroy this world or would you allow it to continue to exist? If everything were destroyed, evil would die out, but what would remain after evil had been eliminated? The result would be total stagnation, exhaustion, and extinction. It would be a world in which prosperity and progress could never exist. We certainly would not want to inhabit that kind of world.

If, on the other hand, we allow this world to continue, we need to purify it. If hell is created in the Real World by negative thoughts generated on earth, we can clean it up only through our own efforts. The only way to purify the earth, while simultaneously aiming for infinite progress and evolution, is to undergo a complete change of mind and bring our will closer to the will of God. This is why you need to settle the account of your life up to this point. Today, make a clean break with your past, and tomorrow begin a new life. Now is the time to pray to achieve this end.

When you pray to God, cut your present life adrift from your past. Pray to be able to make a new start and live according to God's will. Pray with such determination that you will definitely change. If you have made many mistakes in the past and created trouble for other people, either alive or dead, first you need to make amends for those troubles. Then, be reborn and start afresh. This resolution to be reborn will in itself work as an outside divine power. Light from that outside power washes over you, and will bring you salvation.

Do Not Distort the Truth

As we have discussed, there are often thought to be two major paths of spiritual discipline, namely "personal power," or salvation through one's own efforts; and salvation through an "outside," or divine, power. Many people think of these paths as being completely separate. On the path of personal power (or self-power) you discover God or Buddha in the process of refining yourself. The path of outside power involves giving up your own ego and devoting yourself to divine power, in order to achieve enlightenment and happiness.

The Truth is not to be found in either path, yet contains both. They appear to be two separate paths, yet Truth flows through both. Those who do not truly intend to transform themselves will not be blessed with the grace of an outside power. There is essentially no distinction between salvation through self-power and salvation through an outside power—they are two different names for the same doorway to oneness with God.

Once you know that God's blessings and grace cannot be given to those who do not try to change themselves radically, you see that the conventional idea of salvation through outside power has no foundation. This distortion of authentic teachings developed as they were handed down over time. Even if you think you grasp the teachings, in the process of conveying them to others, either self-importance or lack of true understanding can change and distort them. These are the main causes of divisions among religions, and of all the resulting religious conflicts, past and present.

Before encountering God directly through prayer, we need to check and see if there is any danger of yielding to either of these two weaknesses. It is important to make sure that our understanding of the teachings is correct and that we are not using the Truth for our own convenience. These two points are the source of every conflict—past, present, and future.

What will save us from these traps? I envision two primary solutions. The first is an infinite enthusiasm for thoroughly exploring the Truth. Pursue the Truth with your whole heart. Never brandish the Truth as if it were some kind of amulet, or engage in mindless recitation.

The second solution is genuine experience of the overwhelming energy of the Real World, the world of the Absolute, which is also known as the Diamond Realm. Encountering the divine leads to true humility.

Human beings fortify themselves in the citadel called "modern civilization," built of their own power, where they behave as supreme rulers. However, as soon as we come to know the tremendous power of the true world, this citadel collapses. No matter how smart and wise a person may appear to be, that person's knowledge does not amount to even a billionth or a trillionth of God's wisdom. Human abilities are limited and insignificant, yet people tend to be deluded by earthly titles, position, and reputation. Those who have glimpsed the phenomenal world of Truth are truly humble. If you feel that you still have a tendency to take too much pride in yourself or become conceited quite easily, you have not yet come in contact with the world of Truth or experienced its overwhelming energy. The more you know and understand the world of Truth, the smaller you understand yourself to be.

Three Conditions for Prayer

Beauty

Once you perceive that you are no bigger than a grain of sand, you will be able to see with a mind that is pure, clear, and transparent. When you pray in this state, you begin to give out a brilliant light, just like a shining star. There is a mystical glow, an infinitely profound radiance to this brilliance—a beauty. Beauty is what makes faith true faith and what makes prayer true prayer. It proves the authenticity of faith and prayer.

Selfish prayers born of greed are never beautiful, whereas prayers infused with the light of God are divine and stunning. When you want to check whether or not you are praying in the right way, observe yourself to see if you appear beautiful. If you are praying in an egotistical way, will you appear graceful? Look squarely at the contents of your prayer—your words, attitude, and facial expression—as if you were looking at yourself in a mirror, and see if there is beauty in your praying. If you find any ugliness, stop! Do not stand before the gate of prayer; know that you are not ready to pray.

Goodness

Beauty alone isn't enough. Your prayer must also have goodness. So now, ask yourself whether or not your prayer is oriented toward goodness. You will know whether or not your prayer is good if you don't feel embarrassed to write it down for others to read. Just allowing other people to read it is not enough, however. You must also be comfortable having it read by your guardian and guiding spirits, high spirits, or God.

A feeling of shame will accompany a bad prayer; it is the way we judge what is good. When the mind moves away from goodness, you are ashamed and do not want to be seen by others. The fact that we have a sense of shame is itself proof that the mind was created to pursue goodness. Although God has given human beings freedom, he ardently wishes that we will choose goodness. That's why we feel ashamed when we choose otherwise. The nature of your prayers will be revealed when you trust this gauge of goodness.

Love

There is one more condition for prayer: prayer must always be accompanied by love. A prayer without love is not true prayer, but just dead words. Anyone who doesn't have love cannot know God, and anyone who is ignorant of God cannot truly pray. One cannot understand God through knowledge alone; love is essential. The way to God is through love, so the infinite path of prayer is also the infinite path of love. The act of praying exists first and foremost as the manifestation of great love. The human power confined to this three-dimensional physical body is limited. Prayer is what allows this limited power to develop and become infinite.

True prayer is for the sake of love. The purpose of prayer is to contribute your work and efforts for the benefit of others. Prayer allows you to make the most of your life for the sake of many, from those who are alive now to those who will be born in the future. Prayer is synonymous with love. Love is prayer and prayer is love, because God himself is love. Love connects and unites God and human beings. Only those who understand love can truly pray.

What, then, is love? What makes love *true*? We need to understand love more deeply. Love is infinitely good, love is infinitely wonderful; it is infinite joy and infinite enlightenment. To know love is the equivalent of attaining enlightenment. Once you know love, and have established a pathway of love within you, you are able to see all the worlds that God created. To know all the worlds created by God is to be enlightened. This joy of knowing then leads to the next step: the growth and development of love. Knowing leads to enlightenment, and enlightenment leads to the development of love. Enlightenment is the driving force behind the growth of love.

Prayer must be accompanied by beauty, goodness, and love. Prayer that does not express these three elements is not true prayer.

The Power of Prayer

A prayer that fulfills these conditions exerts extraordinary power. In a sense, prayer has the greatest power of all, for it transcends physical existence. High spirits possess tremendous power. If I pray for the creation of an ideal world, that prayer resonates among thousands, even tens of thousands of angels, and they respond to my prayer.

What happens after they respond? Those on earth as well as those in heaven unite to begin all sorts of activities to develop and create a magnificent world. The fruit of prayer is the awakening and arousing of a supreme force, an outside power. Once this power has been generated, the limits of physical existence are transcended.

To conclude this book, I offer a prayer to God.

Prayer for Creating Utopia

Great God,
We thank you from the depths of our hearts
For having given us the valuable opportunity of prayer.

With this opportunity,
May the power of your Love fill the Earth,
May your Light fill Heaven,
May your Glory fill the entire world.
God, please give us strength,
Give us infinite power
And the courage to create Utopia.
May we be able to work in accordance with your will
For the sake of a great ideal,
For the sake of a great creation,
For the sake of a wonderful new world,
For the sake of a new era,
For the sake of the young people
Who will come after us,
And for the sake of future generations.
May this movement of love that we have launched,
This movement to bring happiness to all humankind,
Send out a brilliant light
That shines far into the future.
God, we truly thank you.

RYUHO OKAWA

Notes

Chapter 1. The Principle of Happiness

1. Ryuho Okawa, *The Laws of the Sun* (Brooklyn: Lantern Books, 2004), chapter 6.
2. Ryuho Okawa, *The Golden Laws* (Brooklyn: Lantern Books, 2002), chapter 4.
3. Ryuho Okawa, *The Origin of Love* (Brooklyn: Lantern Books, 2003), chapter 1.

Chapter 4. The Principle of Enlightenment

1. Okawa, *The Laws of the Sun.*
2. Okawa, *The Golden Laws,* chapter 5, section 8.
3. Ibid., chapter 3.
4. Ibid., chapter 1.
5. Okawa, *The Laws of the Sun,* chapter 2; Ryuho Okawa, *The Essence of Buddha* (New York: Time Warner Books, 2002), chapter 2.
6. Okawa, *The Essence of Buddha,* chapter 3.
7. Ryuho Okawa, *The Laws of Eternity* (Brooklyn: Lantern Books, 2001), chapter 5.
8. Okawa, *The Golden Laws,* chapter 3.

Chapter 5. The Principle of Progress

1. Okawa, *The Golden Laws.*
2. Ibid., chapter 1.

Chapter 6. The Principle of Wisdom

1. Okawa, *The Essence of Buddha,* chapter 3.
2. Ibid.
3. Okawa, *An Unshakable Mind* (Brooklyn: Lantern Books, 2003), chapter 1.
4. Ibid., chapter 6.

Chapter 8. The Principle of Salvation

1. Ryuho Okawa, *Tips to Find Happiness* (Brooklyn: Lantern Books, 2004). This book is a collection of question-and-answer sessions.
2. Okawa, *The Essence of Buddha*, chapter 3.
3. Okawa, *The Golden Laws,* chapter 3, section 8.
4. Okawa, *The Laws of the Sun,* chapter 1.
5. Ryuho Okawa, *Love, Nurture, and Forgive* (Brooklyn: Lantern Books, 2002), part 2, section V.

Chapter 9. The Principle of Reflection

1. Okawa, *An Unshakable Mind* and *The Laws of Eternity.*
2. Okawa, *The Laws of the Sun,* chapter 6.

About the Author

Master Ryuho Okawa, born in 1956 in Tokushima, Japan, is the founder of Happy Science. He graduated from the University of Tokyo, and has devoted his life to exploration of the Truth and ways of achieving happiness. In March 1981, he received his higher calling and awakened to the divine part of his consciousness, El Cantare. After working at a major Tokyo-based trading company and studying international finance at the Graduate Center of the City University of New York, he established Happy Science (Kofuku-no-Kagaku in Japanese) in 1986. Since then, he has designed spiritual workshops for people from all walks of life, from teenagers to business executives. He is known for his wisdom, compassion, and commitment to educating people to think and act from a spiritual perspective.

Master Ryuho Okawa has published more than five hundred books, including *The Laws of the Sun, The Golden Laws, The Laws of Eternity, The Laws of Happiness,* and *The Essence of Buddha*. His books have been translated into many languages and have sold millions of copies worldwide. He has also produced successful feature-length films (including animations) based on his works. The members of Happy Science follow the path he teaches, sharing his teachings with those who need or desire assistance.

About
Happy Science

Happy Science is an organization of people who aim to cultivate their souls and deepen their love and wisdom through learning and practicing the teachings (the Truth) of Master Ryuho Okawa. Master Okawa's teachings are based on the "exploration of the Right Mind" and the concrete practice of the modern Fourfold Path in the form of the principles of happiness: love, wisdom, self-reflection, and progress. Happy Science spreads the light of Truth with the intention of creating an ideal world on earth. The teachings of Happy Science are based on the spirit of Buddhism, and integrate the major religions of the world.

Members learn the Truth through books, lectures, and seminars that impart spiritual knowledge about life and the world. They also practice meditation and self-reflection daily, based on the Truth they have learned. In this way they develop a deeper understanding of life, develop character and leadership qualities, and are empowered to contribute to the development of the world.

In addition to his books, Master Ryuho Okawa offers a monthly lecture through his *Happy Science Monthly Messages* publication. For information on courses, seminars, books, and other resources, see Resources, starting on page 174.

Happy Science Contact Information

The official USA website address is
www.happyscience-usa.org
You can request further information on the teachings and activities of
Happy Science at: **inquiry@happy-science.org.**

Happy Science has temples throughout the world. Its main headquarters
are in Tokyo, but its worldwide reach includes temples in the United
States, England, Europe, Canada, Australia, Mexico, Brazil, India,
Korea, Hong Kong, the Philippines, and Uganda. To locate a Happy
Science local agent or temple, go to www.happyscience-usa.org or to one
of the websites listed below.

Tokyo (main headquarters)
1-6-7 Togoshi, Shinagawa, Tokyo 141-0041
Japan
Tel: 81-3-6384-5770 • Fax: 81-3-6384-5776
E-mail: tokyo@happy-science.org
Website: www.kofuku-no-kagaku.or.jp/en

New York
79 Franklin Street, New York, New York 10013
Phone: 1-212-343-7972 • Fax: 1-212-343-7973
E-mail: ny@happy-science.org
Website: www.happyscience-ny.org

Los Angeles
1590 E. Del Mar Boulevard., Pasadena, CA 91106
Phone: 1-626-395-7775 • Fax: 1-626-395-7776
E-mail: la@happy-science.org
Website: www.happyscience-la.org

San Francisco
525 Clinton Street, Redwood City, CA 94062
Phone/Fax: 1-650-363-2777
E-mail: sf@happy-science.org
Website: www.happyscience-sf.org

Hawaii
1221 Kapiolani Boulevard, Suite 920, Honolulu, HI 96814
Phone: 1-808-591-9772 • Fax: 1-808-591-9776
E-mail: hi@happy-science.org
Website: www.happyscience-hi.org

London
3 Margaret Street, London W1W 8RE, United Kingdom
Phone: 44-20-7323-9255 • Fax: 44-20-7323-9344
E-mail: eu@happy-science.org
Website: www.happyscience-eu.org

Australia (Sydney and Melbourne)
Suite 17, 71-77 Penshurst Street, Willoughby, NSW 2068, Australia
Phone: 61-2-9967-0766 • Fax: 61-2-9967-0866
E-mail: sydney@happy-science.org

11 Nicholson Street, Bentleigh, VIC 3204
Phone: 61-3-9557-8477 • Fax: 61-3-9557-8334
E-mail: melbourne@happy-science.org
Website: www.happyscience.org.au

India
Website: www.happyscience-india.org
E-mail: newdelhi@happy-science.org

Resources

Seminars and programs on various topics are provided for seekers on the path of Truth that can help them find keys to solve their problems in life and restore their peace of mind.

Self-Development Programs

Video lectures, meditation seminars and retreats, and study groups are available at local branches. By attending seminars, you will be able to:

- Learn the purpose of life
- Learn the true meaning of love
- Learn how to maintain peace of mind and resist being swayed by anger or anxiety
- Learn how to overcome life challenges, such as difficult relationships with others, sickness, and financial worries
- Understand the workings of the soul and secrets of the mind
- Learn the true meaning of meditation and its methods
- Learn how to create a bright future within your family or at work
- Understand the Laws of success and prosperity
- And more . . .

Happy Science Monthly Messages

Anyone may subscribe to the *Happy Science Monthly Messages,* which contain lectures by Master Ryuho Okawa. Back issues are also available upon request.

Books in English by Master Ryuho Okawa

The Laws of the Sun
The Spiritual Laws and History Governing Past, Present, and Future

The Golden Laws
History through the Eyes of the Eternal Buddha

The Laws of Eternity
Unfolding the Secrets of the Multidimensional Universe

The Starting Point of Happiness
A Practical and Intuitive Guide to Discovering Love, Wisdom, and Faith

Love, Nurture, and Forgive
A Handbook to Add a New Richness to Your Life

An Unshakable Mind
How to Overcome Life's Difficulties

The Origin of Love
On the Beauty of Compassion

Invincible Thinking
There Is No Such Thing as Defeat

Guideposts to Happiness
Prescriptions for a Wonderful Life

The Laws of Happiness
The Four Principles for a Successful Life

Tips to Find Happiness
Creating a Harmonious Home for Your Spouse, Your Children, and Yourself

The Philosophy of Progress
Higher Thinking for Developing Infinite Prosperity

The Essence of Buddha
The Path to Enlightenment

The Challenge of the Mind
A Practical Approach to the Essential Buddhist Teaching of Karma

The Challenge of Enlightenment
Realize Your Inner Potential

Index